THE
NINJA MIND

THE NINJA MIND

KEVIN KEITOSHI CASEY

With a foreword by
STEPHEN K. HAYES

TUTTLE Publishing

Tokyo │Rutland, Vermont│ Singapore

Published by Tuttle Publishing, an imprint of Periplus Editions (HK) Ltd.

www.tuttlepublishing.com

Library of Congress Cataloging-in-Publication Data in process

ISBN 978-4-8053-1273-5

First edition
17 16 15 14 13
10 9 8 7 6 5 4 3 2 1

Printed in Singapore   1307MP

TUTTLE PUBLISHING® is a registered trademark of Tuttle Publishing, a division of Periplus Editions (HK) Ltd.

Distributed by

Asia Pacific
Berkeley Books Pte. Ltd.
61 Tai Seng Avenue #02-12,
Singapore 534167
Tel: (65) 6280-1330
Fax: (65) 6280-6290
Email: inquiries@periplus.com.sg
www.periplus.com

North America, Latin America & Europe
Tuttle Publishing
364 Innovation Drive,
North Clarendon,
VT 05759-9436 U.S.A.
Tel: 1 (802) 773-8930
Fax: 1 (802) 773-6993
Email: info@tuttlepublishing.com
www.tuttlepublishing.com

Japan
Tuttle Publishing
Yaekari Building,
3rd Floor, 5-4-12 Osaki,
Shinagawa-ku, Tokyo 141 0032
Tel: (81) 3 5437-0171
Fax: (81) 3 5437-0755
Email: sales@tuttle.co.jp
www.tuttle.co.jp

The Tuttle Story
"Books to Span the East and West"

Most people are surprised to learn that the world's largest publisher of books on Asia had its humble beginnings in the tiny American state of Vermont. The company's founder, Charles Tuttle, belonged to a New England family steeped in publishing. And his first love was naturally books—especially old and rare editions.

Immediately after WW II, serving in Tokyo under General Douglas MacArthur, Tuttle was tasked with reviving the Japanese publishing industry. He later founded the Charles E. Tuttle Publishing Company, which thrives today as one of the world's leading independent publishers.

Though a westerner, Tuttle was hugely instrumental in bringing a knowledge of Japan and Asia to a world hungry for information about the East. By the time of his death in 1993, Tuttle had published over 6,000 books on Asian culture, history and art—a legacy honored by the Japanese emperor with the "Order of the Sacred Treasure," the highest tribute Japan can bestow upon a non-Japanese.

With a backlist of 1,500 titles, Tuttle Publishing is more active today than at any time in its past—inspired by Charles Tuttle's core mission to publish fine books to span the East and West and provide a greater understanding of each.

Contents

Foreword

When my friend and student Kevin Keitoshi Casey took a deep interest in the ninja *kuji-no-ho*, seemingly magical channeling powers, I warned him that it would not be an easy study. I present a glimpse of these teachings only rarely, because so few are willing and able to grasp this kind of training. I told him that the initiation experiences at the seminars were just the introduction. I also warned him that there would be no such thing as completing the training because it is an ongoing personal evolution. I warned him that mere knowledge was insufficient to work with these powers.

I pointed out that the hunger for this secret knowledge has led many people to speculate or outright lie about how it works. There are many frauds in the world willing to pretend they have attained mastery of such ancient spiritual wisdom. As the subtle truth from authentic training eludes the seeker, he may be driven to grasp at any seeming source of knowledge, no matter how questionable.

Ironically, this passion-driven grasping can close the door permanently on progress, as the seeker latches on to false information and becomes hopelessly distracted by it. It becomes even worse if the seeker then poses prematurely as a teacher, as that person must now justify their confusions to others and further entrench the delusions in their own heart. I was very concerned that my friend Kevin could fall victim to such a fraudulent teacher. I was also reluctantly aware of the compelling ego seduction that could lead to Kevin becoming such a premature, and thereby fraudulent, teacher himself.

The truth is, if a person really wants to pursue secret inner knowledge like the ninja kuji, they will have to hold a difficult balance. The burning passion that drives one to track down spiritual power must be matched with a firm commitment to lessons offered by authentic teachers, practical and grounded research, serious inner inquiry, and a willingness to face awkward and painful personal realizations. It will not be easy, and it will not be comfortable. If a person is only pursuing the kuji to fulfill a fantasy of personal power or illusion of special destiny, they will be turned back when they encounter the true inner obstacles and inevitable personality defects that block the flow of this power.

In my own life, I was certainly inspired by a sense of unfolding destiny as I apprenticed with the ninja grandmaster in Japan, studied his martial art and these seemingly magical nine capabilities, went on to study with *yamabushi* seekers of the mountains' power in Japan, and then gained access to the Dalai Lama and coaching through even deeper realizations by Tibetan masters of the esoteric spiritual tradition in the Himalayas. What is not described in my books is the extreme inconvenience, cost, awkwardness, and even resistance from friends as I pursued this training. Add to that my own moments of doubt, possible arrogance, misunderstanding, and frustration as I unraveled the mystery of what the kuji are. Walking barefoot on hot coals is one literal training experience in the kuji, but also an apt metaphor for the path. It works, but it doesn't always feel safe or comfortable, physically or mentally. The only way to succeed is to keep moving forward with earned faith.

It takes more than one experience with the kuji for the lessons to penetrate and integrate. Way past knowledge, and even past familiarity with the initiation rituals and the feeling of the energy, is a wild land of personal exploration and living the kuji. For that reason, I was so pleased to read Kevin's personal stories of the kuji coming to life for him. He shares the authentic lore, as he interprets it from the layers of understanding revealed along his journey. This personalization is the most authentic way to share the meaning of the kuji.

I am amazed to read how much he remembers of what happened in our times together. I am impressed and a bit surprised to see that he retained those important moments and got the significance. For most of the people at the events he mentions, the memory has long since faded and been forgotten. Kevin really saw the point of what I was teaching. He explored it tenaciously until it made sense to him. I am proud to count such a seeker on the path among my friends and students.

There is an old Tibetan tradition called *terma* treasure-finding, where a seeker who has just the right personal aptitudes and karma connections rediscovers an ancient lost teaching and brings it back to life for everyone. Often the seeker literally finds a physical artifact or text, but sometimes the seeker accesses a teaching transmitted unexplainably through their own mind and destiny. The seeker's way of looking at the world brings the teaching to the surface and gives it a revitalized form for the age.

The Ninja Mind brings to life the first aspect of the nine *kuji-no-ho* powers as reflected from a modern American's adventure. It is a new teaching, because Kevin is interpreting the kuji through his experiences. It is at the same time the original ancient lineage teaching, because it is through our personal challenges and triumphs that these kuji methods live on. He shares the old mantra and mudra that I learned from my teachers on Mt. Yoshino and Mt. Hiei in Japan, he explains how I taught it to him at sacred mountain sites, and then he shares his own reflections on applying the power in the world.

It is his and my hope that you will be inspired to seek out such power in your own life. The journey towards grasping the needed lessons will not be easy. It will not be comfortable or quick or inexpensive. It could be very dangerous. It will never be completed. But it is worth it. We'd like to show you how.

– Stephen K. Hayes

Stephen K. Hayes was the first American to be accepted as a personal student by Masaaki Hatsumi, the thirty-fourth master of the Togakure-ryu ninjutsu tradition. A member of the Black Belt Hall of Fame and the founder of To-Shin Do, a mind and body self-protection system, he lives in Dayton, Ohio. He is the author of numerous books including *The Ninja and Their Secret Fighting Arts* and *The Ninja Defense*.

Martial arts legend Stephen K. Hayes with his friend and student Kevin Keitoshi Casey.
—*Photo by Kim Speek*

CHAPTER 1

The First Encounter

Clad in the traditional white of the Japanese *yamabushi* mountain shamans, I picked my way carefully over the riverside boulders. In future years, this site would be a sacred place known as Shin-Togakure, but that future was forming today. On this day, it was a wild thing, unknown and unnamed to me and the others.

I carefully repeated the power invocation mantra my teacher, Stephen K. Hayes, had taught us the day before. He had given us a mantra of a couple dozen syllables in both Japanese and Sanskrit, and I was determined to retain the exotic sounds long enough to shout them into the waterfall nestled deep in these mountains.

I had searched for a qualified teacher of real-life magic my whole life. I had unexplained psychic experiences from earliest childhood, and I was taught meditation at age seven. I spent my adolescence and early adulthood tracking down various shamans and spiritual teachers, but none of the people I met had the right balance of sanity, authenticity, and spiritual depth to command my attention. Then I met Stephen K. Hayes.

Now I was about to experience an initiation into a truly ancient magical lineage. This was not a New Age religion or a reconstructed rite based on imagination. My newfound teacher had traveled to the last places on Earth that hold this knowledge and trained in traditions with unbroken lineages going back tens of generations.

An Shu Stephen K. Hayes performs consecration ceremonies at the Dragon's Mouth waterfall on Shin-Togakure. —*Photo by Kim Stahl*

I looked out across the small group gathered to take part in the ritual. Most of us trained together at the martial arts school several hours' drive east of these mountains. Some were senior teachers of the ninja tradition, visiting from across the country. Ostensibly, the weekend was a high-level To-Shin Do martial arts seminar granting some insight into the more subtle secrets of the ninja fighting tradition. We got all that—and more.

One by one, we crawled across the rocks to the base of the snow-melt waterfall cascading down. We received final instructions, on how to walk on the slippery rocks, how to breathe in the icy water, and how to handle the impact and cold of the waterfall itself. We were warned that to fall here, so far from medical assistance, could be a life-altering or even life-ending event. We were given the chance to turn back, but I was certainly not about to do that.

A very powerful man stepped into the waterfall ahead of me, a long-time student of Stephen K. Hayes and a great teacher in his own right. He shouted the mantra from beneath the water like some kind of mythological deity, passionate and unperturbed by the force of the experience. "That's what I want to be like," I thought.

Then it was my turn. I stepped forward onto the rocks, carefully balancing. The swift water was destabilizing, but I picked my way carefully to the appointed spot. I repeated the mantra under my breath twice more as I approached, to lock it in. I wanted to say it seven times under the waterfall.

An-Shu Hayes looked me in the eye as I arrived. "Are you ready?" I nodded and then wished I had the voice to speak aloud. He grabbed my hands and I made the shape of the mystical hand posture, the mudra, associated with the practice. He mumbled an invocation over my hands and squeezed them firmly before sending me forward.

I stepped into the waterfall fully intending to shout the mantra like my role model, but my breath was immediately sucked out of me. Despite all the warnings, my own confidence, and my substantial outdoors experience, I lost my bearings and my voice when the water hit my head.

I held the mudra shape with my hands and focused on it so as not to lose myself. I knew a trick, I remembered, and angled my face downward so that I could draw a careful breath of air despite the cascade of water over my head. The noise of the water drumming on my skull obscured all possible outside sound, my eyes were closed, and the cold sent my skin numb. I was cut off from the rest of the universe, immersed in the stream.

When the breath was drawn, I started the mantra. "Namaku…" My breath came out in a squeak. I couldn't even hear myself. I didn't want that. I wanted the world to hear me. I let the breath out with a sigh and carefully drew another, aware that if I didn't make my moment soon, the assistants would haul me out of the water before I passed out.

I held the full breath for a moment and raised my head in the water. I didn't need to bow my head anymore. I shouted the mantra, and I got it out intact. Somehow I found air even in the stream. I drew another breath and shouted it again, louder. I knew that I wasn't going to make it to seven repetitions, so I drew the last breath as deeply as I could and shouted with everything I could muster. I felt the mantra from deep down in my chest cavity, vibrating tangibly beyond mere sound.

I pulled back from the water triumphant, stepped out into the air, and shook my head with a roar. The world came back with the cheers and applause of my friends.

Suddenly, the water wasn't cold anymore. The waterfall seemed small, and I was on the other side of the line, with those who had passed through the experience. Mr. Hayes was there, grinning at me, and I knew I had found my path.

CHAPTER 2

The Nine Powers

Who hasn't wondered whether magic is real?

Advanced staff training on Bear Peak. —*Photo from author's personal collection*

In childhood, we are told amazing tales of human capability. People fly around, heal the sick, read minds, visit fantastic lands, and develop all manner of superpowers that they put to heroic use. Every culture around the world relates such stories, and many of them are remarkably similar in content.

The similarity might just echo basic human needs and hopes, but as we get older, and maybe try to fly a few times, we discover that it's harder than it sounds. It turns out no one we can find is actually capable of such things, or at least not in ways like the stories. Gradually our childhood wonder gives way to a practical and adult mind that knows better than to believe in magic.

Yet, every now and then, a seemingly magical moment slips through. We might see something we don't quite believe, a fleeting glimpse of another time or another's mind. We might witness a momentary feat of strength or speed that seems beyond ordinary human capability, and then rationalize it as an illusion or a special coincidence of physics. We might be touched by a certain cosmic awe or sense of powerful forces beyond the physical, but then assign those experiences to a glitch in our neural chemistry or hand them over to the unknowable forces of religion.

Of course we don't want to surrender our rational thought and sense of causality. It seems culturally, socially, and physically dangerous to do so. At the same time, some of us are never quite willing to let go of that childhood sense of magic. Partially it comforts us, but also at some level it still feels true, fleetingly just out of reach. Just when we've forgotten it or ceased to believe in it, some moment comes along in life that forces us to consider that there could be more to reality than what our conventional five senses perceive.

The situation was the same in old Japan. Legends from incredibly ancient times suggested great untapped powers in the human mind and spirit. Still, the average person saw few miracles performed, and so most people were divided into the faithful and skeptical. The faithful believed in everything, including religious authorities, wise men, snake oil salesmen, and folk remedies. The skeptical had enough piercing intelligence to see through many of the illusions, and drew the conclusion that there was no such thing as magic, or if it did exist, it was long forgotten and unavailable.

The ninja warriors, under extremely heavy pressure from lives of espionage and warfare, certainly were intelligent. Ungrounded superstition would have gotten them killed in short order by very violent and motivated conventional forces. Yet the ninja, operating at the edge of society, witnessed time and again the unusual cases of what a human being can do under pressure. Exposed to such situations, needing every edge they could garner, and free to explore all possibilities, the ninja developed a method of critical inquiry into what we might call magic or psychic powers.

Critical inquiry means they took the old superstitious ways that Japanese shamanism and esoteric Buddhism inherited from Chinese Taoism and they put them to the test. What really works? What powers can be developed? Of what practical use are they?

The ninja were not so much concerned with the ultimate nature of the powers, such as whether they were really magic, gifts from gods, or simply advanced applications of physics. The ninja needed to know what a human being could do, if well trained and well disciplined.

The results were legendary. The ninja accomplished feats thought impossible, and suddenly the ancient stories lived again. The ninja became a force far more powerful than their numbers, wealth, or equipment should have permitted.

One of the systems of studying the possibilities of human power was called the *kuji*. The kuji (literally "nine characters" in Japanese) were mystical symbols that represented a state of mind, a view of life, and a set of skills that worked together to produce extraordinary results. Some of the methods of the kuji look like modern Neuro-Linguistic Programming. There is also a bit of "the power of positive thinking" in there. At higher levels, some of it really looks like magic.

Unconcerned with the mechanics of how it works, the modern student of the kuji can subject their experience and performance to critical inquiry just as the ancient ninja did. A person can learn this form of magic while sacrificing none of their intelligence or education. The opportunity is a dramatically more effective and convenient life, even in daily activities, and the chance for some truly heroic moments.

My teacher Stephen K. Hayes is quick to point out you can't learn the kuji from a book, because the understanding represented by the kuji requires certain experiences. He describes the kuji in his books and DVDs in order to set the stage for the experiences. The description is not the experience, but the description might help you recognize and relate to the experience when it comes along. If these powers intrigue you, you will eventually need to spend time with a qualified teacher who can illuminate the technique, but if you have read, studied, and reflected on these powers beforehand, you'll have an advantage.

CHAPTER 3

The Secrets Told

Twelve years after that first encounter, thousands of hours of training later, my teacher and I were standing together in a Tibetan art shop in my hometown of Boulder, Colorado. He was visiting to teach a seminar on the advanced kuji powers in my own dojo, where I had built a thriving community of 150 students with my wife Mary. We had come a long ways since I hesitantly first approached him in the mountains of North Carolina.

We had just come from the seminar. It had taken me months of convincing him to agree to teach it—that my students were ready for the kuji teaching. He always said that most people weren't ready for the kuji, even though they said they wanted it, so they would miss out on the experience even if it was right in front of them.

The seminar had been a success, and I was ready to ask for more. "I really think these are powerful teachings. The world needs more of this." He simply nodded as he perused the Tibetan *thangka* paintings, so I continued, "You should write a book with more detail about the kuji."

"Actually, I think you should write it," he replied.

I almost dropped the small statue I was holding. "Me? Why would I do it instead of you?"

"I've written a number of books with kuji information in them, and put out several DVDs on the topic. You are very passionate about it. Maybe now it's time for another voice."

I thought about that. It was true that I was the one who had been asking him about the kuji on every possible visit, attending every possible seminar on the topic anywhere in the country for the last 12 years, and reaching out via email, phone, and SKH Forum posts for more information. I was the one who sought out and practiced every piece of kuji-related information, even if it just had kuji in the name and turned out to be unrelated. Passionate was perhaps an understatement.

"How would I do that? Would I just lay out the mudra, the mantra, and the visualizations of the practice?" I asked. "I mean, it's so much more than that. How would I get across the insights, the personal transformation?"

"I think the very best place to start," he began, pinning me with his gaze, "is to tell the stories of our time training together, just like I did in *Ninja and Their Secret Fighting Art*."

Even after all our years together, I still found his gaze intense. I froze under it, until he turned back to look at the art. I remembered reading the book many times, so I mentally reviewed it now. His story came together so naturally and magically when he arrived in Japan in the 1970s. It was like Dr. Hatsumi was just waiting for him, and incredible magical lessons came together right away.

I thought about my own magical lessons with him, unbelievable yet undeniable events that happened. Some of them happened in front of many other people, but somehow I felt like the others might not have noticed or understood the significance.

"When I imagine telling my stories of our time together, I worry that other people will disagree with what happened. After all, these kuji events are so subjective. What if I share my deepest truth and someone else who was there claims no such thing took place?"

"An important question," he acknowledged. "One I have faced many times in my own life. Wonderful real magic happens in the room, and ignorant people claim that nothing happened at all.

Sometimes the most powerful intelligence is just beyond the grasp of the ignorant ones."

He paused and looked at me to make sure I was paying attention. "I call it vajra time. Miracles are happening all around us, right now. Can you see it?"

Stephen K. Hayes and the author visiting a shrine in Nitobe Memorial Garden while traveling for spiritual teachings. —*Photo from author's personal collection*

Our eyes locked and the room seemed to recede around us. The light brightened a little, and the sounds shifted. It was like we had gone into a bubble of some kind, or a protective force field. I had felt it before in our kuji training, but never in a random public place. I didn't know that it was there, just out of sight, at any time. We stayed there for a moment, time suspended, and I thought maybe I had a sense for his thoughts and how he viewed the world.

The bubble burst. I looked around to see if anyone else had noticed—the bored shopkeeper, the listless patrons in the store looking for enlightenment on the cheap. Nothing, no reactions from any of them.

"Ignorant people," he said again, "just don't get it. And they think nothing happened. But you know."

I had never really thought about it from a writer's perspective, so I had always just accepted the ease and clarity of the stories. Thinking about it now, however, I knew it couldn't have been that easy. Now that I had lived through the training, seen the complexity and difficulty of finding truth and transforming the whole self through the experience, I knew that his story must have been much more complex than it sounded in the books.

"What about memories through time? Like an insight that breaks through only after several training experiences, sometimes years apart, or comes together in a seemingly unrelated moment when a phrase in a book or movie delivers the realization?" We had discussed previously how the mind can mysteriously recognize subtle insights out of small clues and artistic reflections. Sometimes the breakthrough comes at the most unlikely of moments.

He nodded. "Those are the deepest ones, aren't they? That's how the kuji work, they deliver themselves to you in mysterious ways, when the time is right. Inner vajra time. You'll find a way to share these truths too." He paused and looked at me. "You have to."

CHAPTER 4

Physical Strength

The Blue Ridge mountains of North Carolina, 2001. "The first kuji, Rin, is about strength," An-Shu Hayes told the assembled training group. Some of us had read his books and therefore knew the name of Kuji One as Rin (臨 in Japanese, pronounced "reen" with slightly rolled "r"). A few even knew the old Chinese Taoist history that explained why the Japanese kanji character, which literally means "face" or "meet," came to represent Strength.

"There are many kinds of strength," An-Shu continued. "And if we were going to study Kuji One deeply, you'd want to look at all of them. But let's start with physical strength, because it is the most clear and maybe the easiest to learn."

Inwardly, I was worried. I didn't want to do a bunch of calisthenics. I was more of a long-distance runner, and not much of a gym guy. Besides, I came to the seminar in the misty mountains of North Carolina to learn magic, not attend a high-school PE class.

As if he read my mind, An-Shu continued with, "Now we could study things like weightlifting to understand strength. That would be the most literal and direct form of the knowledge, and there's nothing wrong with that. But here we're talking about something different. Is it possible that by changing something in our own minds, we could access more physical strength?"

I stood up a little straighter. The group considered his rhetorical question. And then we got our first exercise to experience a taste of Kuji One.

 Exercise One – **The Unbendable Arm**

Get a trusted training partner close to your own size and strength. Your partner is going to be bending your arm while you resist, but there are some safety considerations to setup first.

Face your training partner and place your forearm on their shoulder as in the first illustration. Make sure your elbow is such that it can bend downward (or else you're going to turn this exercise into a dangerous and painful armbar).

Your partner is going to use their two hands to pull down on your elbow and try to bend your arm. Since they get two arms to do it, as well as the leverage of your arm braced on their shoulder, they have a good advantage. Just relax and let them do it gently once to make sure that your arm can bend comfortably that way. Once you have that established, return to the starting position with your arm extended and your forearm on their shoulder.

With this safe setup in place, you can start the exercise. First you will experience their strength while you resist using conventional strength. Tense up your muscles and try to resist, while they use their strength to bend your arm. If you and they are similar in strength, you'll be able to battle them for a few seconds, but they will win out as your arm tires because they have two arms and a better position.

Now for the Kuji One experience. Instead of closing your hand into a fist and tensing up to resist, you will simply place your arm on their shoulder in a firm but relaxed fashion. Open your hand as if you were reaching for something behind them. Although you are going to stay in place, really reach forward, as if a loved one's hand was just out of reach. Breathe out as you reach, imagining your breath coming out of the palm of your hand.

Your training partner will now use their conventional strength to try to bend your arm. When they start putting pressure on your arm, you might be tempted to forget your visualization and focus on fighting them, but for this exercise, keep your mind on reaching for the imaginary hand. Keep breathing deeply and relaxed, imagining the out-breath going out through your palm. Do your best to ignore the person struggling to bend your arm.

You are likely to notice a big difference in the ease with which you resist. If you and the other person are similar in strength, and you follow the directions correctly, you will be able to resist them indefinitely with this method. They will likely exhaust themselves trying to bend your arm and give up in fatigue, frustration, and amazement.

If you are significantly stronger than your training partner, you may find that you are able to resist the arm bend even with conventional strength, but you'll still notice a difference in how easy it is with this method.

If your training partner is much stronger than you, they may be able to defeat your ability to hold the position even with this exercise, but you and they both will notice a big difference in how much force it took to bend that arm.

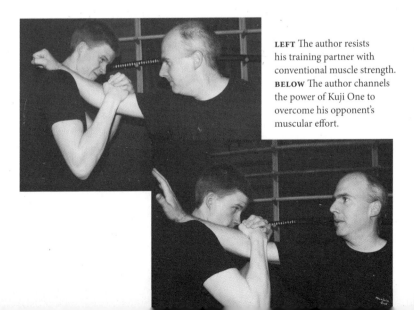

LEFT The author resists his training partner with conventional muscle strength. **BELOW** The author channels the power of Kuji One to overcome his opponent's muscular effort.

"There are limits," An-Shu shared. "How many of you think it's possible for a person to focus their energy and drive their fist right through a wooden board?"

Although To-Shin Do, our martial art, does not practice board-breaking, many people in the group had actually studied Karate or Tae Kwon Do before finding us, so they raised their hands with enthusiasm.

"Of course, because many of you have done it. I've done it too," continued An-Shu. "How many of you think it's possible for a person to lose their focus, slam the same fist into a similar wooden board, and break their hand?" Several of the group raised their hands with a grin, some of them displaying scars and misshapen knuckles from their previous martial art. "So we know that proper mental attitude makes a difference at some level.

"But what about this? How many think it possible that a person could ball up their fist, focus their energy, and shatter a porcelain sink?"

We looked around at each other. We wondered if it was possible. No one had ever seen it done, but we wanted it to be possible. A few of us tentatively raised our hands, trying to indicate our hope that he would show us how to do such a thing.

"I don't know," he said. "I've seen some incredible things in my 40 years in martial arts, but I've never seen that done, and I'm not sure it is possible. And even if it were, what about punching through a car engine block? Or an armored tank? Or a mountain range? There is going to be a limit."

I actually felt disappointed. Ever since childhood, I had wanted to have the power to punch through trees and pick up cars. I wanted to be strong enough to move anything, but I was born as an average size human being. I was looking for magic to take away all the limits.

During a training break later, I got a chance to ask my question in private.

"An-Shu, how do we know what's possible? What if the only reason we can't punch through an engine block is because we believe we can't?"

He smiled generously at my question. "You're right, of course. No one can know for sure what is and is not possible. But it's very important to be real. There is no point in fantasizing about what might be possible. Start where you are, study the methods, and get better. You'll find out what's possible, and when you go further than any of us did, we'll come to your seminar."

It was so practical. It made so much sense. Missing the encouragement in his statement, I flushed with embarrassment that I had shared my childish ideas. "Yes, sir, I will practice."

Of course he knew my thoughts. "No need to be embarrassed. It's normal for the mind to leap far into the future. It's a way for our fears to keep us from actually working on the growth we seek. When you catch yourself, just bring yourself back and get to work on getting better now."

I was amazed. I had never encountered a teacher so knowledgeable of both the topic and the path to mastery. I had never met a man with so much skill who could be so generous with his clumsy students.

My mind was churning with possibilities, and another question finally formed. "So, if board-breaking is something people can learn about Strength now, why don't we do it in To-Shin Do?"

"Because it's not the point of the practice," he said. He got up without another word and walked out onto the mat. It was time for the next exercise.

 Exercise Two – **Getting Earthy**

Get a trusted training partner close to your own size and strength.

You will stand in a natural stance, feet about shoulder's width apart. Your partner's job is to step up behind you, squat low with a straight back, and pick you up with their arms around your waist. Let your partner try it slowly and carefully a couple of times to make sure they can do it without jerking or straining their back. Remind them to lift from the legs.

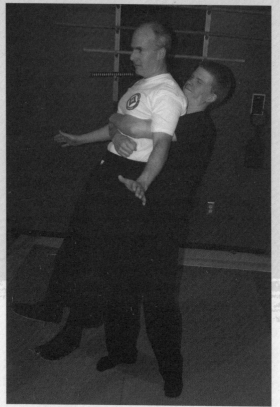

The author stays neutral and allows his training partner to lift him.

The first time, don't do anything special. Just let your partner lift you so that you and they get a sense of how difficult it is for them.

The second time, you will prepare yourself before they attempt the lift. Take a deep breath, and let it out slowly and completely. Imagine yourself as much heavier than normal. Settle your weight into your bones and let your legs soften a bit. Be relaxed and concentrate on your own heaviness.

Let your partner try to pick you up. If you start to get moved or lifted, don't focus on fighting them. Focus instead on relaxing more and getting heavy.

It will make a difference if you can remain relaxed and focused on heaviness. If your partner is very strong, they may

The author gets earthy and his training partner cannot lift him at all.

be able to lift you anyway, but they will feel the difference distinctly. It is like when a parent tries to pick up a child who is passively resisting.

Once you have this trick working for you, try not telling your partner which it will be. See how soon they can feel the difference when they try to lift you.

If you're feeling particularly comfortable with the exercise, you might even be able to activate the heaviness after they've lifted you, and thereby sink back down to the ground against their strength. Be careful, though, because it is possible to hurt your partner if they are not aligned properly for your weight. Take appropriate athletic precautions.

"The patron of the power of Kuji One was called Fudo Myo'o in Japanese lore, or Acalanatha in Sanskrit," An-Shu Hayes explained. "His name means The Immovable One."

I had read about Fudo Myo'o (不動明王) as one of the Five Wisdom Kings known to Japanese Buddhism, certain historical ninja groups, and the yamabushi mountain shamans. I hadn't realized that the image of Fudo Myo'o has existed in ancient India as well under the Sanskrit name Acalanatha.

"We can start with the practice of being physically immovable, but it goes much deeper. Fudo Myo'o also represents how to be imperturbable, unflappable, not distressed by the chaos around you."

I thought of how in the exercises we had practiced, the physical manifestation of immovability was generated by holding my mind to the right thought. If my attention slipped, or I doubted myself, or I let my training partner's struggles distract me, I would immediately lose the ability to resist their power.

"An obvious example of the use of that mental strength is the confidence and focus you can generate to bring strength to your martial arts practice," my teacher continued. "Deeper than that is the ability to hold a space under social and emotional pressure." He looked right at me as he said this, though I wasn't sure why.

I raised my hand. "Do you just mean not backing down?"

He looked slightly irritated at my question. "You could put it in simple terms like that, but in real life it is much more difficult to do with intelligence and grace. When I was providing personal protection for His Holiness the Dalai Lama, we often needed to secure a space for His Holiness, but we were working with monks, spiritual practitioners, celebrities, fans, and media. It would have been totally inappropriate to just get tough and ugly and throw people out like bar bouncers."

The group laughed at the image of the Dalai Lama's protection team roughing up Buddhist monks who had come to pray. An-Shu Hayes nodded at the laughter for a moment, and then suddenly became very serious. "It sounds funny to imagine, but well-meaning people make this mistake all the time. If your idea of strength is mere ignorant resistance, then you have no ability to project intelligent force in the world. In which case, your only choices are to be a doormat or a difficulty."

The room went quiet while we absorbed that. I remembered role-models in my life, good-hearted people, who had either been pushed aside by the insistent needs of others, or who were pushed until they exploded with too much anger and righteousness. I cringed on the inside remembering loved ones who were not able to harness strength in an intelligent and appropriate way.

"So how do we harness the power of Fudo Myo'o?" I finally asked aloud.

Now he smiled at me. "That's the right question. There's a full practice for taking on that energy and power, with a number of safety mechanisms built right in so that you do it in the most positive form possible. Another day, when we have more time, I'd like to walk you through that practice. For today, let's do an extremely condensed version to give a little taste of what it might be like to own that strength."

He folded his hands into an unusual shape. It almost reminded me of a shape we used to make with an old childhood rhyme that went, "This is the church, and this is the steeple… open the doors, and there's all the people."

Forming the mudra (Moo-dra) hand seal associated with the Kuji One power of Strength.

"This special hand shape is called a mudra, sometimes trans-lated as a seal," he explained. "It's used to anchor an idea. We make an unusual shape with our hands that wouldn't come up in ordinary life, and we program that shape by focusing on certain thoughts and energies whenever we make the shape. Later, once we've put enough energy into programming the mudra with the right thoughts, we can go the other way and use the mudra to bring up the thoughts."

Somebody in the group commented that it reminded them of NLP, or Neuro-Linguistic Programming, an approach to anchoring ideas in the mind developed in the 1970s.

"Maybe like that," An-Shu Hayes agreed, "but thousands of years old."

As usual, we fell silent for a moment as he reminded us that while these ancient practices may be echoed in modern attempts to understand the mind, they are far deeper and more thoroughly validated than anything created in the last few decades. I realized what a poor intuitive grasp I had of the scope of time these prac-tices spanned.

"You could think of it like a checking account," An-Shu contin-ued. "You can write a check as big as you want, but you can only cash a check as big as what you have put in the account. Of course, you'll want to start writing checks right away, using the practice to generate strength, but start small and make regular investments to build up your power. Don't try to write a huge check with noth-ing behind it, because all you'll do is damage your own credibility and confidence."

An-Shu came around personally and helped us fold our hands into the correct shape, interlacing the lower two fingers, making entwined rings with the middle fingers and thumbs, and pointing the index fingers forward. "These rings of the middle finger and thumb represent the rope of Fudo Myo'o, with which he binds negative forces and holds them down. The index fingers extended represent his flaming wisdom sword, cutting through obstacles and delusion."

"Take a deep breath in," he said, "and let that oxygen focus your mind on the mudra representing the rope and sword. Release that deep breath, and settle yourself into a more solid and resolute state of mind. Go slowly. Luxuriate in the breath, and build that power."

We went through a series of breaths, slow and deliberate, focusing and settling.

"Good," he said after a few moments. "There is so much more than that, but this is an excellent start. Let's try an exercise."

 Exercise Three – **Manifesting Power**

Get a trusted training partner who can put a little social pressure on you but can remember that they are playing a role to help you practice strength. It is essential that you succeed in the exercise, because the point is to program memories of success into yourself. Therefore, your partner's job is to ensure that you succeed. You probably don't want to try this on your lifelong rival…. Yet.

Preparing to practice Strength.

Start several paces apart, further than you would have a conversation normally. Take a few moments to settle yourself while your partner waits quietly at a distance. If you like, you could try out that mudra, breathing and focusing yourself on a sense of resolute strength.

When you feel ready, let go of any mudra and bring your hands up in front of you in a warning or warding off posture. Let those hands feel strong, palms facing your training partner. The sense is that they cannot move you. You will not pursue or attack them, but you will not allow them to push you.

Your hands coming up signals your partner to begin putting a little social pressure on you. Not physical pressure—just social pressure.

Remember that the point is to build success memories. Your partner's job is to put just enough social pressure on you that you can feel the temptation to cave in or back up, or you are able to hold your ground and stay strong.

Start small. Have your partner just give you a dirty look. Hold your ground.

If that's easy, signal them to say a few mildly rude words, or call you weak. Hold your ground. No need to reply. No need to move, either forward or backward. If you must do something, simply nod slowly and give a small confident smile.

If you are completely succeeding, your partner could even stalk over to you and point their finger at you, or crowd into your space. They are not to touch you in this exercise, so no need to defend or engage them, physically or verbally. Stay confident. Stay strong. Smile slightly and nod slowly when needed.

This exercise is physically simple, but it is not easy.

Hombu Dojo, Dayton, Ohio, 2007: "What concerns me for you, Kevin, is that you are not accustomed to holding firm under the kind of pressure you are going to experience with this project."

An-Shu Hayes and I were sitting alone together at his martial arts school after classes had ended for the night. I was out visiting for advanced martial arts training toward 4th degree black belt, but I had a secret agenda too. I had recently been contacted by the organizers of an upcoming visit by His Holiness the 17th Karmapa, one of the four heads of Tibetan Buddhism. It would be His Holiness' first visit to America in this incarnation and they had asked me to head the security team for his public talk.

Thousands of students of the 16th Karmapa would be there to see him, plus the possibility of protests or worse from Chinese forces because the 17th Karmapa had escaped as a teenager from a carefully groomed life in China. Facing organizing a team of over 60 direct reports to secure a building of over 50,000 square feet, with over 30 entrances and four different security organizations consulting, I knew I was in deep. I turned to my teacher for help based on his experience running personal security for His Holiness the Dalai Lama, particularly during the time that His Holiness won the Nobel Prize in 1989.

An-Shu Hayes was helping me understand that the problem was even bigger than the logistics. "You are very intelligent, so you will no doubt have a good plan. But that won't be enough. Your plan will be undermined by well-meaning and powerful people who have their own desire to make contact with His Holiness. Your plan may even be undermined or overridden by the very people who asked you to make a plan, as they cave under the pressure of politics and money. How will you respond?"

He was speaking from direct experience I knew. Since it was impossible to know exactly what would go wrong, it was impossible to answer his question directly, so I asked a question of my own. "How should I prepare for that kind of pressure?"

He nodded. "The right question. It will be very difficult. To do a good job, to be strong but still diplomatic and intelligent, you will need a strength based in purpose. Your first step is finding and discovering your purpose. Why are you doing this?"

His question surprised me. Why was I doing it? It seemed obvious that when someone offers you such an important position, and the chance to be a part of such a big adventure, you say yes. However, that seemed like a very shallow answer now that it was being consciously examined. It certainly wouldn't be enough to hold fast when confronted by mega-celebrities, powerful politicians, super wealthy patrons and federal agents demanding that I yield.

I then realized that I was doing it to follow in my teacher's footsteps. I had always carried a certain awe that he got to bodyguard for the Dalai Lama, a man I considered one of the greatest spiritual leaders of our time. The adventure, the behind-the-scenes access, and the secret agent power of such a role was a fantasy right out of a movie, and I thought I would never get to have that experience. Suddenly the opportunity had come to me, and I wanted to live a piece of my teacher's story.

Of course, he knew that. Before I could say anything, he continued. "You can't live Stephen Hayes' life. I was the only one who could live the life of Stephen Hayes. Many people try to go back and do what I did, but they can't, because it was a moment in time and space. That moment is gone, replaced with the moment we have now. But you can live your life, and it can be just as big or bigger. So now you have this chance. What are you going to do with it? What does it mean to you?"

His statement was a tremendous gift of acknowledgment and freedom. I was inspired by his life, but I would have to find meaning, contribution, and adventure in my own. I closed my eyes right there at the table and took a deep breath. We had been meditating together for years by now, so he knew what I was doing and I felt comfortable taking a moment.

I tried to clear away all the fantasies and hopes and focus on what felt important about this chance to provide security for the 17th Karmapa. I felt a real connection to Tibetan Buddhism, based on my studies with An-Shu Hayes and the vows I had taken in that lineage. Deep down, it wasn't the celebrity of the Karmapa that was important to me. I knew that I could make a difference in bringing our spiritually-intelligent martial tradition to the scene of His Holiness' teachings. I knew that the world would be a better place if I got involved, because I had the advanced dignitary protection training and real-life experience from my teacher backing me up.

I opened my eyes and found that his eyes were opening at the same moment, seamlessly emerging from meditation with me. "I want to do it because I can make it a better experience for every-one. The Karmapa will teach more easily, the people will learn more easily, and if there are troublemakers, they will be dealt with both more effectively and more compassionately if I am leading the team."

Though I was certain of my answer, I enjoyed the validation of the warm smile that spread across his face. "That's right. That's the motivation that can hold fast. Maybe you can do it."

CHAPTER 5

Mental Strength

Hombu Dojo, Dayton, OH, 2002: "The mind is very responsive to what it perceives," An-Shu told us. "In fact, that's its job, to respond to and make sense of your perceptions."

I remembered detailed studies we had done in the past on how the mind analyzes perceptions and experiences, creating an inner truth to interpret the world.

"One of the things your mind experiences is what comes out of your own mouth," An-Shu continued. "Think about what you say. What worldview does it reinforce?"

"That reminds me of a child who says 'I can't' and proves it true," I commented.

"Yes," said An-Shu, "and when that child turns into an adult, sometimes the story doesn't change. The language may get more complex, but after all the tales of flat tires, dogs that ran away, and factory layoffs, it comes down to the same thing. By focusing on the problems of life, a grown adult can convince themselves of their own inability."

"But there are real problems in life," said another student in the group. "If I lose my job, there are real consequences that may interfere with my ability to do certain things."

"Absolutely!" said the An-Shu. "That is so important to acknowledge. By changing our language, we are not denying cause and effect. We are not pretending that nothing is wrong or that we are unaffected by change. That would be stupid. But there is a difference in how you phrase it."

He changed his voice into a whiny, apologetic character. "See, I lost my job at the factory, and now my ex-wife took all my money in the divorce, and I can't find no work 'cause my back is out..." Several of us smiled at the incongruity of this powerful man taking on the posture and voice of a person struggling with life. We definitely recognized the archetype.

He took on his normal posture and voice again. "Or how about this? I'm searching for work and building my health right now, so I need to delay any major expenditure until I establish my employment. Same core content, but radically different message."

The contrast between the two characters he portrayed was shocking to me. Many times when encountering a person struggling with life, their condition seemed so objectively true. Their slumped posture and sad voice seemed like the only possibility for that person. I could imagine change over time, of course, but it seemed like it would take years. The An-Shu's rapid shift between the two characters made it clear to me that there was nothing physically stopping a person from dropping their defeat in a single instant. They would still have their troubles and ailments, but the defeat could fall away with a mental shift.

Of course, I recognized that the mental shift would be profound, and that may take years if a person is not already a master of their mind.

"An-Shu," I asked, "is there anything we can do to break through the habits of how we describe our lives?"

"There are several things you can do. The first is to become aware of what your habits are. How many of you would agree that you listen to what you would call unhappy or sad music?" Several hands went up. "Okay, so given that, how many of you like being sad?"

No one put their hand up, but there was a hesitation in the room. "When I'm sad, I like listening to sad music," said one person.

"Why do you think that is?" An-Shu Hayes asked.

"Well… it feels good to sort of indulge the feeling, I guess."

"I think that's true," he replied, "and that's why some people spend time reinforcing a feeling that they don't really want."

I thought about my own tendency to seek out music that reflected my feelings, and then indulge in amplifying those feelings. I recognized a sense of justification in the process. It felt good to validate, celebrate, and intensify whatever I was feeling. An-Shu's comment raised the question of whether that was strategically intelligent.

An-Shu smiled as we thought it over, and then set us on an exercise to experience our own habitual stories.

 Exercise Four – **Noticing Your Story**

Get a trusted training partner who will hear your story and reflect back what they heard. Explain the exercise to your partner before you begin.

Sit down a few feet apart, facing each other. You are going to tell a story about a difficulty you encountered in life. It's best if it was disruptive but somewhat trivial, on the scale of a flat tire, a missed airplane connection, or an awkward job interview. The point is to find a story where you cared about the results, but it was not deeply traumatic.

You have approximately two minutes to tell the story. Do your best to find the level of detail that will take about two minutes to tell. Twenty seconds is too short. Ten minutes is too long.

Your partner is going to just sit and listen. They are not going to say anything. If possible, they are not even going to nod or agree in any way. They are simply going to devote their full, rapt attention to you for two minutes.

When your story is done, your partner is going to say, "This is what I thought I heard." They then have two minutes to tell the story back to you, just the way they heard it.

Your job is to listen to them raptly for two minutes. Look for what they emphasize. What came across to them as the main points? What seemed important to them, from the way you told the story? Is that what you think really was important?

Remember that the point is not about the accuracy of their re-telling. The point is for you to use your training partner as a mirror, reflecting back to you what the world hears when you tell your story. You may be tempted to think that your training partner just "got it wrong," but just for this exercise, entertain the possibility that something about your posture, voice, tone, or persona communicated the story that way.

An-Shu brought us back from the exercise as we mulled over what our partner reflected to us. "Once you get good at this exercise with a partner, you can do both halves of the exercise yourself, recognizing your own story even as it comes out of you. You can do this out in your life, at work or with your family, and no one will even know that you're doing it. That's a powerful form of practice toward creating the correct story in your mind. What did you notice in this exercise?"

I wanted to object to what I heard reflected back to me. "There were some things my partner reflected that were not really how I felt. I mean, I did say them, but they didn't match the real me."

"So why do you think you said them?"

It was an obvious question, but it made me stop. "I think... I didn't want to seem arrogant in the story."

"Okay, good. So we don't know your story, but what you're telling me is that because you were concerned with how you might be perceived, you changed the story. You made the story be something that did not reflect your deeper truth. And in the changed version of the story, instead of arrogant, what were you?"

"Afraid," I replied.

"But you really weren't afraid when it happened?"

"I should have been afraid, but I really wasn't. I was just sort of concerned and annoyed. But I thought it would sound arrogant to say that I wasn't afraid."

I fell silent, and the air in the room seemed to thicken as the point of the exercise started to dawn on me. An-Shu let a few moments pass and then gave it words. "So, you created and told a story of fear in yourself. You even told yourself that you should have been afraid. How do you think that is likely to influence your mind in the future?"

I felt sick. I did not answer, taking it as a rhetorical question. After all the times in my life I had indignantly cast off other people's opinions of me, I was horrified to see that I was unconsciously sabotaging my own inner strength. I could see that I had been creating fear in my life because I felt like I should be afraid. The silence went on too long, and I realized that he was still waiting for some answer.

"It almost seems like I believe in my feelings so strongly that I don't really notice them as habits," I said.

"That's exactly right. Feelings seem to happen to us, caused by outside forces, but in fact, we've set ourselves up by the way we tell our story as we go along. So, is it possible to take charge of that process? To notice our habitual story and start telling the story we want to experience?"

I sure hoped it was possible. "So, we have to make the unconscious conscious?" I asked.

"Yes, that's part of it. And we have to practice retelling the story our way."

"Isn't that just 'wearing rose-colored glasses' and pretending everything is good?" I pressed. Although I liked the idea of optimism, being realistic and authentic was important to me.

"Profoundly different," he asserted with a touch of fierceness. "We are not ignoring difficulty when we retell the story. We are not hiding from the challenge of life, or pretending that we are somehow above cause and effect. We are telling a story of bravely engaging the challenge of life."

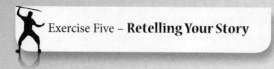

Exercise Five – **Retelling Your Story**

You can try this out, building off of Exercise Four.

As before, you and your training partner will sit a few feet apart. You will tell your story in two minutes, but this time your task is to make the story as heroic and epic as possible without changing any material details. Tell the story where your motivation is as positive as possible, and the setbacks are legendary challenges that you engage with heroic zeal.

Explain the exercise to your partner before you begin, so that you and they know that you will be speaking in unusually heroic terms. This will help alleviate any embarrassment or tendency to downplay your own power. Just for this exercise, it is your job to paint yourself as powerfully as possible.

As before, your partner will then mirror back to you what they heard in two minutes. They will not make fun of you—they will celebrate and reflect your heroic version of the story.

As an example, if the original story went…

> "So there I was, trying to get through the morning commute, and I heard this noise. I realized I had a flat tire. It sucked. I had to pull over in traffic, in the rain, and trudge around trying to find the tools in the back. I got all dirty and sweaty trying to change the tire, got to work 30 minutes late, and the first thing my co-workers noticed was how bad I looked."

> The upgraded story goes…

> "So there I was, battling for position in a sea of steel and anger, when disaster struck. One of the tires lost pressure, and the car was dragged to the side. I knew I had mere moments to avert even greater damage, so I swiftly checked my mirrors, assessed the situation, and found my opening. Guiding the car deftly to the shoulder, I secured the vehicle

and leapt into the stormy weather. I acquired the tools I would need, concealed in the trunk, and positioned myself for optimum leverage. The task was Herculean, but the car was lifted and the backup tire installed safely. Once I was back in the driver's seat, I checked the time and realized I could still make it to the staff meeting. I roared off in my repaired vehicle, and arrived at the office to the concern and wonder of my co-workers as they noted the battle wear on my clothes."

Notice how you feel after re-telling the story in heroic fashion. How does that change your feelings about such a story coming up again in the future? How does that change your feelings about who you are?

If the heroic version feels a bit false at first, it may be because you are not used to framing your life in such a fashion. Ask yourself—are the details true? Is this interpretation any less valid than any other?

"An-Shu," I asked, "how does a heroic inner story relate to our ability to project strength into the world?"

He nodded. "In our To-Shin Do martial arts practice, some people will scoff at a black belt. They might say, 'What, you think some black cloth tied around your waist is going to help you in a street fight?' But they don't understand. It is not the black cloth itself, but the confidence and identity that the wearer gained on the way to earning it. You think confidence and identifying with winning doesn't help in a fight? It makes a huge difference. So, yes, that black cloth tied around your waist is going to help you a lot in a real fight, because it reminds you of your power. It's so powerful, in fact, that it can even help you when you're not wearing it."

"So, by believing in ourselves, we can accomplish whatever we want?" I said, trying to summarize.

"No." He frowned at me. "Belief alone does not overcome cause and effect. It is not magic in that way. If a person believed in their skill when they had none, they would still not get far. However, a person with skill who does not believe in it… that person also does not get far. Belief unlocks the capability that we really do have."

"But how far does it go? If I believe strongly enough that I can walk through walls, could I do it?"

"That is not my experience. I won't close the door on any possibility, because I have seen some amazing things in my time, but I've never seen someone walk through a wall, punch through a mountain, or pick up a building. No one can say what the outer limits are, but that kind of speculation is a distraction from the point. Build your inner vision of heroic truth by telling what you have accomplished in a heroic way. The truth of your life is miraculous enough, if only you will let yourself see it that way."

Looking back, that was an extremely valuable lesson that I wasn't ready to understand. I really wanted comic book style magic. Feeling confident was all well and good, but I wanted supernatural powers. I wanted to punch through mountains. I didn't yet see the tremendous satisfaction and happiness to be gained in life through a heroic inner narrative, nor did I understand that no capability, no matter how great, intrinsically creates happiness. We must craft happiness artfully and consciously.

That seminar ended without any demonstrations of fantastic feats, and as I drove several hours back to our home at the time in North Carolina, I imagined what I would like to see. I realized that I really did not expect or believe in the extremes of comic-book strength, where Superman picks up an entire commercial jet. However, I wanted something more than just inner confidence and an unbendable arm. How would this Kuji One skill show up in actual application?

I was helping my friend move when I got my first answer. He had trained in Kuji One with An-Shu Hayes many times over a ten year period, though we had not discussed it much. For some reason, his old townhome had the washing machine on the second floor, and I was helping him carry it down the staircase. This old beast of an appliance had been a struggle for the two of us to lift up out of the utility closet, and we were sweating as we moved it down the hallway to the stairs. We took a breather there and then started the dangerous part.

We were about one-third of the way down the stairs, with him on the bottom side, when his feet slipped out from under him. Everything went into adrenaline time. He started to tumble down the stairs, letting go of his side of the washing machine. I tried my best to hold on to the thing from the top, slamming it into the wall to try to stop it from falling on him. There was no way I could do it—my grip was completely wrong to stop it from pulling forward, and it was far too heavy.

My attempt to slow the fall of the appliance caused a gap to open up between my friend and the steel beast. When I finally lost control of it a second later, it tipped out into space above the stairs rather than sliding down near my feet. The next thing I knew, the washing machine was totally airborne, a few feet over my friend's head. My attempt to control it had turned it into a lethal missile.

My friend looked up and saw the situation. There was no time to dodge and nowhere to go. I saw him take a deep breath, and something hard to define rippled through his body like a wave. He was not a big guy, but he seemed to become denser and immensely sure of himself. He stood up into a low squat on the lower stairs, placed his hands above his head, and literally caught the washing machine.

I couldn't believe what I had just witnessed. Time seemed to stop. There he was, holding an entire washing machine over his head, perfectly still. His muscles were bulging, but his body was perfectly aligned, the model of ideal strength. He reminded me of some kind of heroic statue.

I stared for what may have been several seconds before he reminded me of his suspended humanity with the words, "Help me!" I rushed down and took a strong position on the stairs above, so he could tip the washing machine into my control. I took careful possession of it on the stairs, pinned it to the wall with my body weight, and declared that I had it.

He released the energy from his body. The wave rolled back through him with a big exhale and he became human again.

I heard him whisper a mantra to himself, the sounds from an ancient form of Sanskrit used to anchor these powers.

"What just happened?" I said, though I knew it was the power of Kuji One in action.

"Fudo Myo'o did not fail me," he replied.

I spent the months after that developing my ability to call up the confidence and the sense of the power that I had witnessed in my friend and in training exercises with An-Shu. I mostly used it to open stuck jars, pick up heavy objects, and move downed trees on my land in North Carolina. I discovered I could take a deep breath, focus on my memories of the sensation of strength, and channel that to manifest strength much more powerfully than I was normally able.

It was a good feeling, and I thought further training would make it even stronger, so I continued to travel back to my teacher's dojo in Dayton, OH whenever special training on the topic was offered. I also looked for hints of the power during our more usual black belt training sessions there, hoping to catch a glimpse and steal some more insight into this Kuji strength.

I was serving as An-Shu's demonstration partner in a black belt training session when I got my chance. I held a wooden pistol in my hand, pointed at my teacher's head, while I simulated holding him hostage. We had paused the action for a moment while he explained the essential point of moving offline with subtle and surprising timing so that the pistol-wielding adversary (me) did not have the chance to notice or process the change. He was presenting this very advanced martial arts concept carefully so that no one would think it was as simple as "snatch the gun."

Having next showed how he could trick my natural reactions into going the wrong way and losing my aim, he took hold of the gun that I still had and created a mild wrist lock as a simple mechanical example of what one might do next. The emphasis was not on the mechanics of the take-down since the room was filled with black belts. We all nodded in understanding, excited to try out the subtle misdirection method.

Then, while he held the gun in my hand and everyone assumed the action was over, I felt something subtly shift. I don't know if I felt it physically through the gun, or I heard his breathing change, but somehow I felt that rising focus energy from him and I recognized it from practicing Kuji One. In my own practice, I usually needed to stop moving, close my eyes, and focus for several distinct seconds before I could start to call up the power, but I felt the power rising in him in the span of a heartbeat, with no overt physical shift.

Fascinated, I turned to look at him, but there was nothing special to see with my physical eyes. He seemed to just be standing there, paused, but I felt the energy take over the gun and then my hand. My fascination turned to fear as the energy raced up my arm and seemed to invade my body.

"Or you could just do this," he commented lightly. No one in the room but me knew anything was happening. "DOWN!" he suddenly shouted with great force.

My body seemed to decide on its own to obey him rather than me. I felt my muscles throw myself on the floor involuntarily, and I felt like a passenger in my own flesh. Half a second later, I was on the floor and I had released the gun to him. There was no wrist lock or arm bar. There was no trip or throw. There was no physical pain or coercion of any kind. Somehow I had involuntarily volunteered to give up.

Although he has a very powerful presence, it was not mere social intimidation. At this point, we had worked together for some years, and I was braced to bring my spirit to the training exercise. It was clear to me that something more significant had happened.

Everyone in the room assumed there had been a subtle wrist lock or balance taking that they simply missed, which was not uncommon with An-Shu's techniques, and so they simply nodded and found training partners to work on the misdirection of aim that was the purpose of the exercise.

I shook off my bewilderment, jumped to my feet, and hurried to ask my question before he went off to coach individual training groups. "An-Shu, what did you do there?"

"Just a simple wrist lock," he replied.

"But you didn't apply the wrist lock. That's not what took me down. There was some kind of energy," I protested.

"Oh, that," he smiled, as if it were a minor matter. "That's just *ki*."

I was surprised to hear him use that word, ki, because when I had asked questions in public about ki he usually reframed the question to avoid such terms and instead focus on positioning and timing. Now he was using the same term to lightly acknowledge my profound experience.

"How so?" I prompted. I had learned by now that the best way to get information was to keep my questions short and simple.

"Just like when you pick up a sword, and you send your breath and awareness down the length of the sword, you can do that to a limb when you need to affect it."

I contemplated that idea, based on my sword experiences. There is indeed a big difference between holding a sword, swinging a sword, and wielding a sword. It's hard to capture the feeling and movement difference with language, but truly thinking of the sword like your own arm, as an extension of your body, allows a natural confidence in movement. Such ability is usually the result of long hours with the sword, where one's identity of owning the sword gradually seeps in through athletic endeavor.

To invoke that natural confidence and power in a heartbeat, through another human being, was an application of the power that had never occurred to me. I wondered at the idea of "wielding the attacker."

I took too long thinking about it, and he patted me on the shoulder and moved on to assist those training. For the rest of the session, I was obsessed with observing this projection of *ki* in various techniques. Though we were nominally training in techniques for second-degree black belt, through dignitary protection scenarios, I was training in Kuji One.

I came to realize that for An-Shu, this ability was simply integrated into his way of being, like an energy muscle that he could contract and relax automatically when needed or desired. I wanted that impressive and magical ability, and I could see that it was more than merely understanding the technique of sending ki energy. Just like how the mechanical takedown on the gun disarm was only rendered viable by the more subtle positioning that led to the opportunity, ki projection could only matter if the mental state was rapidly available in the context of life. The technique itself could be learned through the Unbendable Arm exercise or other similar things, but the cultivated at-will ability was another level of integration.

Now I realized why he usually redirected the topic when I asked in public. It would be far too easy to think that the ki energy itself was the point, and miss the inner work that makes it useful.

I still had no idea what that inner work was, however.

After training ended for the day, I waited around until I could catch my teacher alone for a moment. "An-Shu," I asked, "how do you get to where you can project ki so effectively on demand? Is it simply a matter of practice and time?" I hoped there was a secret he could give me to accelerate the process.

"That is a factor," he agreed. "All skill and wisdom comes down to two things. Live a long time, and pay lots of attention. The first part you can't do anything to accelerate, so cultivate patience and health so you can make it. But for the second part, there is a lot you can do, and most people don't do enough."

"I paid attention today. I saw something, and I don't want to let it go."

"That's good," he replied. "That desire is what carries us forward. The desire could cause you to suffer, of course, which is why you also need patience as you develop skill. But that same desire can also appear as an energy that makes things happen."

I appreciated the motivational point, but it didn't seem to solve my question at hand. I knew plenty of people who wanted the power, talked about such things, and had been around the martial arts for a long time but did not seem to have anything approaching this ability. I knew it was possible to live a long time, train hard, try to pay attention, and still fail utterly to comprehend. "Yes, but… how do I actually learn this power?"

"You are not paying attention," he said.

"What?" I was totally confused. He had my full and total attention in this conversation and throughout the weekend. How could I possibly have paid more attention than my total obsession with the topic, based on my compelling experience with him?

"I just gave you the answer, and you asked the question again, which means you didn't get it. And, you didn't understand that you didn't understand. You thought you got it, when you really got nothing."

My brain locked up trying to understand what I didn't understand. I took pride in being intelligent, so it was incomprehensible to me that I could fail to get it even when devoting my full attention to it. I backtracked the conversation carefully, recalling each word in the last few exchanges. I talked aloud to clarify my thoughts. "Desire carries us forward. Desire is energy moving us toward our goals. Somehow that's my answer to how to develop instinctive ki projection."

It slipped in to my mind that I had taken his statements as general life advice, interpreting desire energy as social or inspirational energy that gets me out of bed in the morning and has me working on my tasks. But what if he meant that desire could manifest literally as ki energy?

He must have seen some of this dawning on me. "Now you're paying attention," he said. "Go back to the hotel, and keep paying attention. Tomorrow we'll open with an exercise to add to it."

Exercise Six – **Transcendent Intention**

Start by finding a place where you can sit and think without interruption.

Think of something that you really want in your life. If you had a magic wand, and you could only use it to create some personal benefit, what would you ask for? You can't ask for world peace or an end to all suffering, but you can ask for a new car, a new ally, a new job... some kind of simple and direct request that would help you and make the world a better place if you had it.

Once you think you have it, close your eyes. Let yourself take a few deep breaths and relax.

Your first step is to focus on the desire. Give yourself a few minutes to consider...
- How will this thing make my life better?
- How do I know I really want it? What does it feel like to want it?
- How much do I want it? What am I willing to endure to get it?

The second step is to analyze it. Take a few minutes and contemplate...
- What needs to happen to make my desire come true?
- How can I make those things happen?
- What allies, resources, or circumstances would bring my desire to fruition?

The third step is to verbalize it. Spend a few minutes considering...
- How could I phrase what I want in as direct and simple terms as possible?
- Who should I tell about what I want to motivate myself to go after it?
- Who should I ask for help in achieving what I want?

The fourth step is to visualize it. Enjoy a few minutes imagining...
- How will I know when I have achieved it?
- What will it look like when I have achieved it?
- What will it feel like when I have achieved it?

If you have a friend assisting you, they can read each of these steps to you. It is not necessary for you to answer the friend out loud, although you may if you wish. However, you might be more honest with yourself just to hear the questions and let your thoughts run freely in your own mind.

"Come on back to the center of the room," An-Shu announced as we concluded the exercise.

I had received some intense realizations of what I wanted in life, and what my unconscious motivations and fears were. I was amazed to realize that I was not really pursuing some of what I thought I wanted. There were indeed steps I could take to bring my desires to reality, if only I was brave enough to own and take those steps.

However, he had told me privately the night before that this exercise would be relevant to my question about ki projection. I wasn't seeing the connection yet, so I was looking for a way to ask my private question in the public venue.

Before I could do so, someone else asked how this exercise applied to martial arts training. He nodded and replied, "There is an idea in the esoteric mind tradition called transcendent intention, where your desire becomes a focused intention so powerful that you can overcome obstacles that would logically have blocked you from your goal. Can anyone here see how that could help in martial arts?"

We all nodded. At the very least, passion for training could allow a person to overcome distance, financial difficulty, and time pressures to make sure that they still got the training they wanted. Certainly that was my story, driving eight hours each way every month to Ohio from North Carolina so that I could access these mystical teachings directly with An-Shu.

I wanted to ask directly if this was my answer to developing instantaneous intuitive ki projection, but I couldn't ask without sidetracking a group that was not in my private conversation with him the night before. My first thought was to ask him later in private again, but as I soon as I thought it, sharp words formed in my mind. *Don't ask later – pay attention now!* I looked up to see if he had sent me that thought, since it seemed like what he would say if he had access to my inner monologue. He was already answering another question, however.

I forced myself to try to think it through on my own. Going back to my memory of the gun-disarm moment, I could see how An-Shu allowed himself to feel strongly in that moment, and then channeled that emotional energy using his breath and body alignment to affect me. I could see that it was effective. Why was it so strange to me?

It struck me that I had a belief that a really tough martial arts master wouldn't be emotionally touched by an attacker. I had subconsciously been aiming to be above emotion in a fight, because that seemed cleaner and more pure. Now I had to realize that not only was the idea unrealistic, but it was also limiting my ability to channel my power.

Of course, losing control of myself due to emotion wouldn't be helpful, but I was now seeing how different that was from trying to avoid having emotions. If the power of projecting energy to influence or even control an attacker were driven by desire and transcendent intention, then emotions definitely would have a role to play. It was only my fear of my own feelings that had driven me to construct a transcendent fantasy instead of honing transcendent intention.

I snapped back to the conversations in progress in the room. "There is an inner teacher," An-Shu shared, "separate from and more subtle than the outer teacher. The outer teacher takes a human form and explains things to you, and this is extremely helpful, especially in the beginning. But you can become complacent, asking the teacher instead of reflecting on your own experiences and trying things out. The inner teacher is sometimes harder to find, but can give you more subtle and nuanced answers as well. Develop the skill of searching and analyzing your thoughts, memories, and emotions. Then you'll have better questions for the outer teacher, and get that much more out of our precious time together."

"An-Shu," I asked, "you said that being too reliant on the outer teacher can make you complacent and cause you not to develop critical thinking skills. Is there a similar trap in being too reliant on the inner teacher?"

He nodded. "Of course. Someone too reliant on the inner teacher insists on reinventing the wheel. Instead of using the wisdom of their teachers and seniors, they are constantly questioning issues that have already been well-resolved."

"But isn't it good to derive those answers yourself, to understand them more deeply?" I argued.

"Good, now you know which trap you are more likely to fall into," he commented with a smile. I blushed a bit at the accuracy of his observation as he continued. "Yes, there is value in verifying for yourself. Our lineage teachers have always recommended that. There is value in faith in your teacher, and our lineage teachers have always recommended that as well. There is no contradiction, if you are big enough to hold it."

He gave us a moment to take that in, and then continued. "It is also the case that some outer teachings, things the teacher says, only get unlocked years later. You may hear a teaching, and not really understand it, or only partially understand it. You may even think you did understand it, when in fact, you were missing the point. It goes up on a storage shelf in your mind for years, and then one day, an experience comes along. If you are open to it, that teaching can come to life as the experience connects with it. The outer and inner teacher work together this way to deliver some of the most important lessons."

I remembered that there was plenty of life wisdom I had heard from my parents in childhood that made no sense at the time, but came into focus in my college years or as I was settling into my engineering career as a young adult.

"If something doesn't make sense now," An-Shu concluded, "listen to it carefully so that you have the wisdom for later, when the time is right. Then put it on the shelf and don't worry about it. It will come to the surface when it is supposed to, as long as you are paying attention." He seemed to give me a secret glance with that last statement.

As I drove back to North Carolina with my wife, we had plenty of time to discuss these ideas. We both had many examples of wisdom that took years to come to the surface, so we could relate to the idea of the inner teacher processing things over time.

We also had stories of channeled emotion leading to extraordinary results. One friend was in a car that crashed on the highway, flipped, and caught fire. He crawled out of the wreckage and dragged his friends out of the car, but one of them had gotten pinned under the vehicle. He remembers the emotion of realizing that she was going to burn if he couldn't get her out, and that energy took over his body and he literally lifted the car off of her.

I always enjoyed such stories of incredibly heroic mythical feats, but I didn't know how to categorize them or how someone could turn on that ability if they needed it. It always seemed random and circumstantial when it was accessed. Now I could understand it as a form of ki projection, enabled by channeled emotion called transcendent intention. Somehow, giving it words made it more tangible and learnable.

Not long after this trip, I encountered some criticism of my teacher on the Internet. In an attempt to belittle To-Shin Do as a martial art, the anonymous critic was saying that the dojo was actually partly an acting school, because the training includes learning to take on the role of attacker with posture, voice, and attitude. To-Shin Do also asks people to use their voice in return while defending, shouting "Stop!" or "Hey!" The critic was uncomfortable with voice and emotion as part of the martial arts process, preferring to focus on mechanical technique only.

I too felt uncomfortable with those things when I first started training, but I adjusted to them as part of To-Shin culture. Now, years later, I was finally understanding the purpose. Voice and emotion channel intention, and developed intention amplifies the power of the mechanical techniques. It can be uncomfortable for social reasons, but also because channeling feelings when you are used to suppressing feelings seems like losing control.

On the other hand, who doesn't want the power to amplify technique and direct the attacker with your will?

Mountains of North Carolina, Kuji One training with An-Shu Hayes: "There are some magic words you can use to remind yourself of this power. These magic words affect your mind when you hear them and when you say them. The words are in an ancient language, a language ancient even to our Japanese ancestors hundreds of years ago. They come to Japan from China, and to China from India, but even in India thousands of years ago, these were not the words of the marketplace. They were used to call up our inner power and describe that which we want to embody."

I sat near the front of the small group of students, enthralled. I wanted to know the magic words. I also carried some doubt. Could ancient words really hold power, like in a fantasy novel? "An-Shu," I asked, "is it the words that make the power, or is it our training and associating the feeling with the words?"

"Possibly both," he replied. "Certainly a big part of it is our training, and putting our memories on these words so that we can come back to this powerful moment when we need it. For that reason, it is helpful that the words be in this ancient Sanskrit, so that we would never use them casually in life and diminish their power that way."

I nodded, remembering how we used a special hand-seal to anchor the memory in a similar way. It was important that the mudra hand-seal be specific enough that we wouldn't do it unintentionally and make it ordinary.

"However," he continued, "there may be some power in the fact that these words have been spoken by seekers like us for thousands of years, across continents and oceans, through war and peace, in so many cultures. There may be some of their sincerity and desire bound to these words across time, if you can accept that. With no practice or effort from us, that might not mean much, but it may help our practice."

It made sense to me. I could not believe that the words recited by a robot, or a person acting like a robot, would do anything all by themselves. On the other hand, I remembered how certain songs seemed to have magic in them even the first time I heard them, when I had no memories or associations yet. It did seem possible to me that some cultural energy can get stored in certain songs, phrases, or words.

In music, there is also the truth that certain sound combinations evoke certain emotions. Certain sounds imply sadness, happiness, power, or freedom. I wondered if there might be a science of sorts behind the construction of these Sanskrit phrases, just as there is with music.

An-Shu Hayes continued his explanation. "These magic phrases in Sanskrit are called mantra. His Holiness the Dalai Lama translates mantra as 'mind-protector,' something which fills your mind and keeps it from thoughts that will drag you down. Imagine it! When you need strength, confidence, focus, and channeled intention, is it possible that doubt, distraction, or delusion could sneak in there? You know it's possible. A mantra held in your mind, possibly spoken with your mouth, keeps you on track, focused on the power you need in that moment. It takes out all the space for doubt to creep in, and so your best power can come forward."

I realized that many athletes do this instinctively, with a fight song, or even an exhortation to "Go! Go! Go!" That kind of fast yell, to build the spirit, channel emotion, and focus on winning, was a modern kind of mantra. What we were about to learn was just that much more sophisticated, developed by masters of the mind across millennia and tested across cultures, space, and time.

An-Shu distributed small slips of paper with the mantra written on them, in original Sanskrit and the Japanese-accented form of Sanskrit that he learned in the Buddhist lineage in Japan.

"If you like, you can learn this. It's a little tricky to get the sounds in your mind, so I'll give you a short form of the mantra that you can use. The literal translation of the words I will give you later, but it is not terribly important right now, because this is symbolic language designed to cut through confusion in the mind and burn away any cobwebs. Let's try this out together."

Carefully, one word at a time, he took us through the Japanese-accented form of the mantra to get the pronunciation correct. Slowly, a kind of rhythm emerged as we got accustomed to the strange sounds, and though we were still reading off the slips of paper, we could feel something communicated deeply through the words.

Namah samanta-vajrânâm canda mahârosana sphotaya hûm
trat hâm mâm (Sanskrit)
Namaku samanda bazaradan senda maka roshina sowataya un
tarata kan man (Japanese accented)

Once we got into a group rhythm with slowly saying the mantra over and over, I noticed An-Shu Hayes switched to the Sanskrit form, pacing it alongside our Japanese form. Where the Japanese had clear consonants and vowels, creating a reassuring beat and rhythm, the Sanskrit had a breathy and slippery quality, like smoke floating around the solid beams of our Japanese staccato. It was clearly the same words, the same sounds, the same intentions and energy, but with an older and even more mystical sense about it.

Eventually, the time was right for us to finish. I don't know how we all knew. No one rang a bell or announced anything, but we could feel the energy start to settle. We all knew which iteration of the mantra was the last one, and we all concluded at once, sinking into a profound silence. It had gone from dusk to night while we chanted, and the silence and darkness wrapped around us in the woods like a bubble.

"Can you feel it?" An-Shu Hayes said quietly, but we all heard him. "This is vajra time."

It felt like time had stopped, or we had somehow fallen out of time as we normally know it. I don't know how long we sat there, motionless and silent, or whether that is even a meaningful question. We definitely felt something, but it would have been hard for anyone to find words. Certainly no one could speak aloud at the moment.

And then, just as with the mantra, we seemed to all know when the moment had passed. People began to stir gently. A few moments later, we were getting to our feet. An-Shu directed us to return to our campsites on our own time, and let the significance of the moment linger for as long as possible.

I was stunned. How could it be that a group of us chanting some strange sounds in the woods could transport us so dramatically? I was not surprised that we felt some emotion, but the effect seemed to go beyond the psychological. I had never felt that feeling of being outside time from music or meditation. Even if I chalked the feeling up to my own inner trance-like state, how did we all know when to stop? How did we coordinate so seamlessly, even though it was new to all of us and we were not communicating by any normal means?

My mind went to images of druids gathered at Stonehenge or wizards attending some magic ritual. I couldn't understand the mechanism of what had happened, but the experience was overwhelming and undeniable. Something has passed between all of us in that moment, something that reached inside of us and communicated to us. I had a deep feeling, like an almost-remembered dream, that the mantra had communicated with parts of me not normally accessed, parts of me so far below my normal consciousness that I couldn't even get to the memories.

The next morning, An-Shu called us together in the misty woods for further details on how to use the mantra.

"As I mentioned with this mudra hand posture," he said, folding his hands into the Kuji One seal, "one form of practice is to anchor a memory or an emotion to the practice. We can do that with the mantra too, forming strong memories and intentions while saying the mantra, and then that feeling is available to us later if we recite the mantra in a similar fashion. You could, if you like, say the mantra while folding your hands into this shape, anchoring to both at the same time. That makes for powerful practice."

I wanted powerful practice. I folded my hands into the mudra and stared down at it, remembering the feelings from the night before and running the mantra through my mind. I had spent my evening hours memorizing it so that I would be able to practice with it today.

"It's also possible," An-Shu continued, "to have a short form of the mantra that reminds you of the longer phrase. Even better if that short form can have a connection to your own culture and time, so that it can activate powerful memories from your own life."

"The last two words of this Kuji One mantra can be used as a short form to remind you of the whole phrase. You do have to get the sound right. K-A-N M-A-N, but it's not 'garbage can man'. It rhymes with 'gone' or 'lawn'. It's the dawn of brawn. KAN MAN! Say it with me a few times. KAN MAN!" We followed his lead, and he continued. "KAN MAN! KAN MAN!"

As we continued, the consonants of the phrase started to drift and blur a little with each repetition. "KAN MAN!" turned into "KAMMAN!" which then further morphed over several cycles into "KAM-AN!" I realized that An-Shu Hayes was doing that on purpose, slowly bending the sound so that it retained the powerful exclamatory mantra quality but took on slightly different consonants in our pronunciation.

"KAM-AN!" we shouted together. "KAM-AN! KAM-AN! KAM-ON! KAM-ON!"

Finally he revealed where he was going by shouting "Come on!" in English, but with that same mantra quality of voice. We joined him in shouting "Come on! Come on!" and then he switched back to "KAN MAN!" Some of us joined him on that, others kept at "Come on!" and some were shouting a hybrid in between.

The combined voices, each with their own pronunciation, created something new. There was a chaos to the sound at the surface level, because each voice was slightly different, but my mind connected the similarities too and the group voice that emerged was a powerful essence of the mantra that was deeper than the individual sounds. It became clear that the true mantra was a feeling and a rhythm of the shout. It might take a shifting form from one moment to the next, but the true voice was clear.

An-Shu Hayes' voice became louder in the mix and rose up to a high point, and then dropped away suddenly. Somehow we knew that meant that the mantra was done, and our various voices fell away.

"Good!" he said. "That's important. That's how we bring that mantra to life. And isn't it remarkable that our own culture has this voice hidden in the phrase 'Come on!' Somehow the truth speaks to us even without training, but training lets us recognize it."

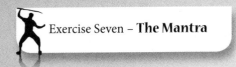 Exercise Seven – **The Mantra**

You'll probably want a place where you can speak or even shout without being heard or feeling self-conscious about it.

Remember that unlike in standard English, these sounds are pronounced consistently based on the spelling.

"A" will always be "ah" as in "lawn"

"E" will always be "eh" as in "get"

"I" will always be "ee" as in "free"

"O" will always be "o" as in "no"

"U" will always be "oo" as in "boot"

With that in mind, you can sound out the mantra. Take your time at first, picking your way over the sounds carefully.

NAMAKU

SAMANDA

BAZARADAN

SENDA

MAKA

ROSHINA

SOWATAYA

UN TARATA

KAN MAN

Once you get comfortable with the individual words, you can try saying it all in a single sentence, like a chant. Let the words roll out evenly, drawing out the vowels a little bit.

You could also try a more evocative voice, like the way a stage magician says "Abracadabra!" before revealing his trick. Have fun with it. See how it feels.

When you have found a way that you can voice it with passion and feeling, you can try it out with the mudra hand-posture as well. Imagine yourself as a powerful and focused being. The more you can call up a sense of power while you do it, the stronger it will be for you.

August, 2002, mountains of North Carolina: I was due to test for my Shodan 1st Degree Black Belt that evening, but I had been horribly sick all day. As I lay in my tent, drugged on cold medications just so I could breathe, I wondered if I would really be able to rally and hike down to the circle in the woods where the testing would happen.

Some part of me must have decided that I wouldn't give up easily, because the next thing I knew, I was standing at the circle's edge as the crowd gathered and the lanterns were lit. Someone was asking me if I was sure I was up to it, and I nodded, not even knowing to whom I was speaking.

My wife and three other friends were testing with me. One by one they called us out for free-response, where teams of five people would attack randomly, unarmed or with training knives. My wife went first. As soon as she stepped into the circle, one of black belts jumped on her back and pulled her into a choke. She spun him over her shoulder and slammed him into the muddy ground. Another man tried to punch her and she jumped back, grabbed his arm, and twisted it into a shoulder lock. One by one the black belts assembled put her to the test.

The energy was palpable, and the crowd was cheering her name and applauding. I was enjoying seeing her power and precision, even though I was personally feeling terrible.

Then something shifted. Someone in the crowd shouted the short form mantra we had been practicing earlier that day. "KAN MAN!" I felt my pulse pound once. "KAN MAN!" someone else said, and then spontaneously, the magic phrase started popping up all over the group. "KAN MAN! KAN MAN!" the crowd voice chanted, falling into synchronization.

My wife grew more powerful. She became more stable, stronger, and almost seemed to have increased in density and substantiality. The last man to attack her was much larger than her, stabbing down on her from above with a wooden training knife, and yet his attack seemed to happen in absurd slow-motion. She easily stepped out of the way of the descending threat, took his balance, and deposited him on the earth.

Then it was over. The crowd applauded, and it was my turn.

Someone helped me to my feet and gave me one last "Are you sure?" look. I nodded to the unspoken question, took a deep breath to rally, and stepped into the circle hoping I looked strong.

The crowd began the chant right away. "KAN MAN! KAN MAN! KAN MAN!" I felt the energy moving through me, reinforcing muscles that had gone without food for almost two days. I became aware of my bones and the substance of my physical body, and I felt solid. *I can do this,* I thought.

The one leading the ritual called out for the first team to approach, and they rushed into the circle. A sense of alarm coursed through my nerves. I didn't feel ready. I was still finding my ground. My mind was reeling from illness, adrenaline, and the chant energy. Everything seemed to be happening both fast and slow—I could see every detail unfolding, but like a dream, I couldn't seem to move or respond at the same pace as events. The first attacker closed the gap to me, moving very quickly, and I realized it was one of the teachers from our dojo, a very skilled man I knew well.

His fist connected with my nose. I had barely responded to his first attack, moving just enough that my nose didn't quite break, but certainly not defending. Pain and shame washed through me for a moment, but as those feelings sank into the pit of my stomach, as I was staggering backwards from the impact, something woke up deep inside. I felt fire in my belly. Sounds like a metaphor, but it didn't feel metaphorical at all. It felt like a fireball of energy, warmth, power, and passion inside my guts.

The chant penetrated my thoughts. "KAN MAN!" I heard in my head, much louder than the pain or shame. "Come on!" my heart echoed back.

It was all inside of a split second. This friend and teacher was already throwing his second punch, doing his best to make this experience as real as possible. Power surged through my limbs from the fireball in my guts and the mantra in my heart. I spun with his second attack, grabbed his arm, and threw him. It wasn't like a martial arts throw, where you get someone's balance and upend them. I threw him with supernatural force, like throwing a man-sized Frisbee. This much bigger man left the ground and flew across the clearing toward the cliff at the edge of the mountain, unable to stop himself. One of the senior teachers observing invoked his own supernatural powers and leapt ten feet from his chair to intercept my attacker mid-air and pull him back to earth before he went over the edge. They stabilized together right on the edge.

I would be shocked later, but there were four more attackers closing on me even as that unfolded. "KAN MAN!" the crowd chanted. Now that the first explosive release had occurred, shaking off all of the doubt and confusion from getting hit, the surge of power was alive in me. I was super strong, super confident, and totally awake.

The next four were dispatched with ease. Team two was launched, five attackers with knives. Out of character for my usual self, my confidence did not waver in the face of this pressure. It was not the sense that I couldn't be hit or hurt. It was the surety that getting hit didn't matter. I was more powerful than the circumstances, and I had already overcome being hit. I was feeding off the crowd energy, the power of the mantra, and the new force awakened within.

With no fear, I could see everything as it unfolded. Video analysis of the test later showed that techniques were unfolding at a rate of five moves per second, but inside the flow, each movement felt deliberate and informed by the balance and timing.

I never felt fatigue. Team three launched, and a few seconds later, they were all covered in mud from the well-trampled ground in the circle.

"KAN MAN! KAN MAN! KAN MAN!" the crowd chanted, and then burst into cheers and applause. I was breathing heavily when it ended, but it felt like a bellows feeding a forge rather than the desperate gasping of exertion. I snorted and grunted, shaking my head as I left the circle. I was somewhere beyond words, but it felt good and powerful.

My others friends proceeded through the experience themselves, each performing beyond normal capacity as the power of the group voice carried the mantra into their hearts. "KAN MAN!" I roared alongside, sending my surge of energy and adrenaline out with my voice and into the night air to bolster my friends.

When it was done, the chants and the noise subsided. An energized heaviness settled over the clearing, and we realized just how dark it was in these woods. One of the Coleman lanterns had failed sometime during the test, and now the other one sputtered out. One of the helpers jumped up to fix it, but An-Shu Hayes waved him off.

"Make no mistake," he said quietly, but every last soul could hear him. "Something very unusual, very important has happened tonight in these woods. It's not just us here."

Chills ran up my spine as he spoke, in a thrilling way. There was indeed the sense of unseen ones watching, dozens if not hundreds, peering in on us from the woods and even the sky above. I wondered who exactly they were, but I felt like I could almost see their swords and armor from another time.

One by one he called us forward. Our black belts manifested from somewhere in the darkness, snapped a few times to dissipate the dust that had settled while they waited for us during our long years of training.

When he called me up, it seemed as though all sound ceased, everywhere in all of time. I was not deaf, as I could hear my footsteps and my heartbeat, the snap of the belt fabric, but somehow those were the only sounds. No leaves rustled, no one moved in the group, not a single throat cleared. The sound of the belt snapping fell into a vast space built out of the highly witnessed darkness and silence.

I placed my previous belt, my last *kyu*-rank colored belt, around my neck as An-Shu Hayes blessed my personal black belt with a mumbled mantra and a sword mudra. He wrapped the belt around my waist, prepared the knot in the front, and then indicated that our dojo's senior teacher, Dr. Richard Stack, should take one end of the belt while he took the other. Some kind of look and energy moved between them, and then without words, they moved as a single unit, both pulling on the two ends of the belt and tightening the knot with a spirited shout into the night. Their voices went into the belt knot and sealed it. I was a To-Shin Do black belt, and this place would remember this moment.

Dr. Stack invited us up to celebrate at his personal retreat, a massive log cabin home overlooking a million acres of the Pisgah National Forest. We gathered there to process the energies and congratulate each other. Our group was the first formal group of students from the dojo going to black belt, and so our instructors felt a certain pride as well to know they had guided us to this moment.

One of the instructors caught up with me privately there. "Kevin, I just wanted to let you know how amazed I am that we get to celebrate this moment together. When we met you and Mary... well, to be honest, we really didn't think you'd be here today."

Sounds funny, but I understood. I was a computer engineer, and she was an administrative assistant at a school of social work. We did not manifest powerfully at all when we walked into the dojo. The teachers, by contrast, had all come up under very harsh training. They were nearly all police officers, prison guards, and soldiers who had seen the worst and lived through it. Even just talking to them terrified me in the beginning.

Because of their life experiences and their deep respect for the lineage, they made absolutely sure that we were worthy of a black belt in the martial art that they called their own. It was rigorous. It was scary. It took mental strength.

I realized that the mantra, that "KAN MAN!" activated and drew upon every decision I had needed to make over the years. It brought to the surface every time I got scared and took another step forward, and made use of all that energy as a power. Though I sometimes feared things that my teachers seemed to find quite easy, what I now realized was that the process of moving ahead in the face of fear was the real definition of the inner mental strength we would seek. My own fears, conquered, set the stage, and now here I was accomplishing something on a scale far beyond what I could have imagined in the beginning. Even the war-weary warriors had acknowledged my power.

KAN MAN, indeed. The moment of a lifetime, defined by a lifetime in a moment.

We made our way down to the lower level of the home, where an elegant private dojo had been constructed. An-Shu Hayes and other senior teachers were there, talking lightly. I hesitated at the threshold before such great ones, but the mantra whispered through my mind again and encouraged me. I stepped into the room and joined them.

Somehow, I found myself standing by the beautiful *kamiza*, the spirit-shelf focal point of the dojo with lineage pictures and special items. An-Shu Hayes was standing beside me, and though a few others were nearby, he turned to me and they all fell away as if on cue. Suddenly we had a moment of privacy in the midst of a group. *How does he do that?* I wondered.

"Kevin, I know you are interested in some of these deeper practices and the items associated with them. There is a kind of ritual wand called a vajra that I heard you were looking to acquire."

The diamond-thunderbolt wand known as a vajra, representing indestructible truth.

A *vajra* (Sanskrit) is also known as a *dorje* (Tibetan). The Japanese word, *dokko*, is rarely used. I perked up. They are unusual items in most places, and I had been searching for one for some time. The wand is associated with insight into the ultimate form of truth, and is used as an object to focus meditation on that topic. However, the practices themselves are also kept secret and require training from an advanced teacher.

I thought An-Shu Hayes might tell me where I could get one. Instead, he reached up onto the *kamiza* and revealed a *vajra* that had been concealed there. He brought it down and showed it to me. "These usually come in a set, with a bell, but I acquired this one under special circumstances years ago in Nepal."

I looked at it in awe. It seemed very old, and the metal seemed to glow with magic. I wondered what kind of stories this artifact carried. *What were these special circumstances?* Before I could ask, he went on.

"I'd like you to have it."

My mouth hung open in shock. I blinked a couple of times. *He is giving me the artifact?* "Thank you," I finally stammered. I looked around to see if anyone else was witnessing this. Where were the dojo teachers? Where were my fellow black belt testers? Does this kind of thing usually happen as part of a black belt test?

There was no one nearby. The few people in the vast room were in their own conversations, far away enough to be unaware of my moment. It was just for me.

"Thank you," I said again. It seemed insufficient, but the only possible thing to say.

He put a hand on my shoulder, smiled, and said, "May you enjoy where it leads you."

The most powerful experiences in the world can open the soul to new possibilities, but if there is no follow-up, the power fades. Fortunately, not long after being initiated into the potential power of the mantra, I got a chance to try it out away from my teacher.

My wife and I lived then on four acres of wooded land with a long gravel drive providing access to the house. As we went to leave one morning we found that an overnight ice storm had bent one of the younger pine trees into a graceful arc that occupied the road, blocking the only way out. Though it was a young enough tree to bend, it was substantial at a foot in diameter and perhaps 30 feet in length.

I stopped the car, got out, and approached the tree, trying to move it by just shoving at the base. No way. Even my full-strength efforts caused it to yield only slightly. My wife and I debated and decided that we would use some rope and try to pull the tree back to vertical and tie it in that position.

I tied the rope around the top of the tree (easy to reach because it was bent down) and walked into the woods to pull. I could barely budge it. My wife joined me, but even pulling together, the tree was not lifting. We got a steel pole, planted one end in the ground, and tied the rope to the middle so we could pull on the pole like a giant lever with better grip and amplified power. The tree was still too heavy.

Now we remembered the mantra practice. We sat down in the woods, centered ourselves, and made the mudra hand-posture shape with our hands. We went through the long form of the mantra that we had both memorized, quietly at first and then building up power. As we went, I felt an inner stirring from my memories of training with An-Shu Hayes and the power of the black belt testing. The power started as a memory, and then built into a confident feeling deep in my core. As we kept up with the mantra, the confident feeling turned into a kind of heat that radiated out from my center into my limbs, and I recognized the feeling of ki projection I had experienced from my teacher.

I felt stronger. Much stronger. I still didn't know if we would be capable of lifting the tree, but I felt three times as powerful as before.

We had both gone into the state, and the air felt thicker around us from all the energy we had charged up. We stopped the mantra at the same time, and when we made eye contact, we could both tell we were in that same place of Kuji One power.

We took hold of the steel pole without a word and started to pull. I quickly reached the limit of my usual strength, as before, and the tree was not moving, but I found a whole reserve of power somehow under or behind my usual strength. We surged with power and the tree started to yield.

The tree top lifted several feet and the tree started to unwind a bit from its arc, but as it did so, we were needing to lift more and more of the tree's weight. The relatively light top moved, but the middle section needed to uncurl as well. Our progress stalled against the heavier resistance, and we hung there for a moment, holding a great deal of weight but unable to progress.

We dug in deeper. We lined up our bones and muscles in the way our physical martial arts training had taught us. We breathed deeply, and the mantra came out on the whispers of the exhale. I felt my feet sink a few inches into the earth from the enormous pressure on our bodies as we pulled on the steel lever against the rope. It seemed like we might be defeated, but there was a fierceness inside that wouldn't accept it. I was determined either to lift the tree or snap the rope.

The mantra dissolved into a guttural growl, and I felt that heat in my core blazing like a bonfire. The intensity of the burning rolled down my limbs and I found even more power than I would have thought possible. The force was so intense that I wondered briefly if my bones could hold up to it.

They did, and as we growled at the tree, it groaned in response and finally yielded. Wood fibers cracked as the tree straightened and the limbs tore free of other trees where they had become entangled. Once the tree was vertical, the force was still strong but lessened, so we were able to pull our feet out of the depressions we had dug into the earth. Keeping the tension, we gradually walked the rope around a stronger and older tree and tied it off, securing the young one for future growth.

We released the rope and the energy. We were sweaty, but not exhausted. I felt alive and powerful. We celebrated with a high-five and then noticed the steel pole. The two-inch diameter pole was bent and carried dents from our hands. We looked down at our small hands, that now seemed so powerful, and smiled.

I was never the same after that. The experience with my teacher was an initiation into a new power, and it took permanent root in me after we claimed it with the tree. Suddenly I could turn on that power by simply focusing for several seconds and whispering the mantra. Stuck jars in the kitchen, heavy gear in the garage, and equipment in the lab at work all yielded to the technique time and again.

For the first time in my life, I felt genuinely strong. I could move things that bigger people could not, because I knew how to channel my strength. I felt like I really had it.

Life would illustrate that there was more, however.

A few weeks later, we went canoeing on a local river with a friend. We had some experience, but the river had recently flooded. A few hours into our journey, we lost control and accidentally flipped the canoe as we made a fast turn. We all tumbled into some light rapids.

This was not particularly worrisome as we had all experienced it before. You pop up, orient your feet downstream so you can catch any incoming rocks, and try to figure out where the canoe is. The water was about three feet deep and fast moving.

Unfortunately, there was a large tree that had fallen across the river and completely blocked our channel. We were swept toward the tree and in peril of being forced under it and pinned down there by the strong current. I had been pinned underwater like that once before, as well as rescued my own mother from such a scary situation, so I was keenly aware of the danger. I shouted for everyone to get on their feet and brace against the horizontal tree trunk so we could climb out.

One by one, we were swept into the tree, and we all managed to brace against it and get our feet down in a stable position. The water was pushing against us forcefully, but we were stable as long as we stayed braced. We collected ourselves for a moment and checked in—everyone was okay. It was a perilous position, but I knew we could get to shore safely as long as we took our time and moved deliberately on our way out of the current.

Then I saw the canoe heading toward us.

An empty canoe only weighs about 50 pounds, so even if it's moving fast, a strong person can snag it or catch it. What many inexperienced canoeists don't realize is that a canoe full of water weighs in the neighborhood of 1000 pounds. It may only be going 10 mph, but it's going to hit very, very hard.

The three of us were already pinned to this tree trunk by the current and braced out. We couldn't stop bracing or we'd be swept underwater and trapped in the branches. We couldn't move quickly, but that canoe was going to crush us against the tree. There was nowhere to go.

We had about three seconds to prepare. I yelled "Stop the canoe!" and we did our best. We put our arms out and tried to catch it, but it overwhelmed all three of us and slammed our torsos into the tree. I was bounced off the canoe and the tree and then ejected from the collision. Our other friend had a similar situation on the other side, but my wife was pinned right in the center.

Amazingly, none of us lost our footing, so for a moment, I thought we were okay. Then my wife started screaming. The force of the current was grinding the thousand pound canoe into her, gradually crushing her against the tree. She was pushing as hard as she could to get it off of her, but to no avail.

The other two of us rushed to the edges of the canoe and started pushing back, but we couldn't move it. There was no time for a mantra, no time to get into a meditative state and call up a past memory. My wife was being actively injured now, and each fraction of a second was hurting her more.

Instead of a memory gradually turning into a burn that led to power, it was like a bomb went off inside me. The immediacy of the situation overrode any hesitations or need to get into the proper state of mind. Her voice, wordlessly expressing the sounds of urgency and pain, became the mantra that powerfully activated and focused my desire to get the canoe off of her right now. Her screams of pain activated the Kuji One power inside of me instantly, and ki energy flowed through me.

The same power that took several minutes to develop when pulling on the tree surged out of me in that single heartbeat, and both the canoe and the river were overcome. Suddenly I was able to push the broadside canoe upstream and walk against the current in total defiance. A part of me observing from the back of my mind thought it impossible, even as I was doing it anyway. I shouted "Move!" as I forced the canoe off of her, across the channel and to the bank. I was commanding the canoe, her, the river, and the whole situation to change. She pushed off the tree and forded the current to the shore.

Although it had been painful, she did not have any broken bones or organ damage. She would recover in a few minutes. As we collected ourselves on the shore, the power ebbed and I came back to my normal self. I had experienced one answer to the question I had put to my teacher: how are desire, voice, and ki energy related? I had experienced the surge of mental and physical strength that came with the urgency and commitment of a loved one threatened.

In the deceptive way of rivers, from the shore the water now looked peaceful and beautiful. I reflected on what had just transpired.

There is so much more going on here than meets the eye. The river looks safe but can be lethal. I look small but I can be strong. The canoe looks light but becomes heavy. What looks impossible one moment is instinctive the next.

I felt a keen disconnect between appearances and reality. I realized that when things happen fast, the perspective I held made all the difference. There was no time to get the right perspective. I remembered that as a kid, before I could drive, I sincerely thought that I didn't need to wear a seat belt because if I saw us getting in an accident, I would just put my seat belt on. It was an absurd thought, but I couldn't understand that until my first car wreck at age 16, when I learned firsthand the speed of such things. I got the correct perspective.

My sense that I understood the Kuji One Strength power had been built on a similarly incomplete understanding. Now I was seeing that the power of channeling my strength relied on a certain perspective and attitude. The mudra and the mantra, calling up my memories of success, was a way to get in touch with that perspective and practice it. However, they wouldn't be enough under pressure. There wouldn't be time and space in certain situations to call up success.

In this case, my love for my wife, and her expression of pain, galvanized me and cut through any slowness or reluctance, and I was able to act. But what if I had gotten frozen? Or what if she hadn't vocalized her pain? What if I needed that power to act and channel my will, but no one was there to motivate me?

I could see now that if I wanted to be able to rely on this Kuji One, this inner strength channeling, I needed to know how to wear that power all the time. I needed it as a perspective of power that I carried through my minutes and days. How could I develop that?

Thus I had a new question for my teacher.

CHAPTER 6

Spirit Strength

"It comes in stages," An-Shu Hayes told me. "First, you have to identify with the possibility of developing this power. You have to come to suspect that it exists, see examples of it, and want to have the experience."

I remembered the early stages of my training, where I wondered what was possible. My thoughts about Kuji One then were a constant mix of hope, doubt, fantasy, and fear.

He continued. "Then you have an initiation or an empowerment, a moment where the teacher helps you experience the power for the first time. That opens the door, because you have a memory of success."

"But you can still doubt somehow that your experience was real," I countered. "I doubted at times. I wondered if it was just a cognitive illusion, a circumstance. I wondered if it was luck, or if you and the other people just set me up to have a magical fantasy but nothing really happened. It wasn't until I had my own experiences out in the world, over and over, that I started to be really sure that something was going on."

"Absolutely right," he replied. "There's no way around that. You have to take the empowerment and then go explore it and practice. Eventually, you not only know that the power can exist, but you know that you can do it sometimes. It takes time to get used to that idea. In the esoteric training tradition, where this lore was passed on, the power is represented by the image of a deity. The image is a way to identify with what it would look like to own the power completely."

I had asked the question on a break at one of the group training seminars in Dayton, but others were starting to tune in to the conversation. The group was coalescing around our discussion.

An-Shu Hayes shifted voice to address the group. "We were just discussing the traditional Asian image of strength. This Fudo Myo'o character, the powerful blue-skinned wrathful king surrounded by flames, represents something in old Asian culture, through India, China, Tibet, and Japan. He had different names in each place, but the iconography stayed fairly consistent across cultures and centuries."

He went on. "The idea was to have something where you could ask yourself, 'What would it be like to be that powerful?' That way you could imagine that you were actually that way. We've probably all done this naturally at some point, as children. You pretend to be the hero from a movie or a comic book, and for a moment, the pretending actually does grant you a little more confidence and commitment. Now imagine an adult version of that."

"An-Shu," one student remarked, "is this like, 'fake it 'til you make it'?"

"Could be," he acknowledged. "Do you think it's possible that by pretending to be confident, you may actually find some confidence?"

We all nodded, some smiling at their own memories of having done so. "But what about false confidence? Bravado? Faking it to hide from fear?" asked another student.

"Yes, there is such a thing. It might even be a necessary stage to go through." An-Shu Hayes paused to let that sink in for a moment. "And then, what if we went beyond pretending? What if we went beyond the imagination of childhood and took on an actual visualization of power?"

Visualization sounded like a different word than imagination. "Athletes visualize success before a big game, or a big attempt on a difficult maneuver. I guess we wouldn't call that pretending or faking."

"Exactly," An-Shu agreed, pointing a finger at me to emphasize it. "They know they are capable of it, because they have won before. They are calling up that winning power again, identifying with their capability of winning."

I was struck by the possibility of the imagination games of childhood, so easily dismissed as useless dreaming and fantasy, being a capability that could be transformed into the deepest form of spiritual practice.

"Now let me ask this," said my teacher. "Do you think it's possible to do the opposite? Even though you have won before, do you think it's possible in a given moment to identify more with the possibility of losing?"

We all nodded. We had all proven that to ourselves at some point.

"So if that is true," he continued, "then you can see the value of identifying with strength and victory. You can see that it really does make a difference, no matter what stage of development you have reached."

"Maybe this is me identifying with failing," said one student, "but sometimes it seems like I don't really choose whether to identify with success or failure. It seems like it chooses me, like I can't help how it looks."

An-Shu nodded. "Yes. That can be true. Before we can direct ourselves to identify with success, we need some basic stability of mind. We need to develop the capability to direct the mind at all, before we can choose a certain target for it. That's where foundational meditation skills come in, and that's why the ancient traditions that guard this training always start there."

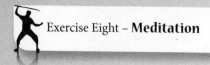

Exercise Eight – **Meditation**

Find a quiet place where you won't be interrupted. If finding a quiet place is hard in your life, you can play some centering music or even just white noise like a fan to cover up outside sounds a bit and help you focus.

Meditation is fundamentally about the ability to place your mind where you want it, and keep it there. Too little energy, and you will fall asleep or daydream. Too much energy, and intrusive thoughts will take over and make you feel like you need to jump up and do other things. Meditation is a kind of mental balance between falling below and leaping above the ability to pay attention.

Just like physical balance, you can and should practice developing mental balance throughout your life. There is no such thing as "achieving permanent balance," because balance is by definition the skill of responding to circumstances in just the right way. You can't achieve it and be done with it, because as soon as you do, things change.

However, you can get very good at recognizing when you are in balance and when you aren't. You can also get very good at getting back in balance when you've lost it. That is the goal of meditation.

Depending on your temperament and circumstances, there are many ways to practice meditation.

There are many informational resources in the world to suggest methods. Here is one method.

Sit comfortably with your back straight. A straight back helps you stay focused and alert.

Rest your hands someplace comfortable.

Take a few initial deep breaths to settle in.

Adjust your posture again now that you are somewhat relaxed. Keep the back straight.

Either close your eyes, or soften your gaze so as to stay relaxed.

Focus your mind on a single positive image. Just hold the image in your mind.

Outdoor meditation is especially refreshing.

If you notice at some point that you have forgotten or changed the image, just refresh it.

Even just five minutes of practice is very beneficial. You will feel yourself shift gears in those five minutes, and new ideas and clarity may arise. It is common, especially in the beginning, for those new ideas to break you out of meditation. You might keep a notebook handy nearby when you practice so that you can write the idea down and then forget about it. Eventually, you'll be able to just let those ideas go without even writing them down.

If you practice every day, you will definitely get better. You will find it easier to hold your mind to something, whether it be a conversation, a work task, or just waiting patiently. No matter what your religious or spiritual outlook, there are great benefits to being able to direct your mind.

As you get more comfortable with the technique, you may find yourself naturally lengthening the practice time. If you can get to 20 minutes of practice at holding focus, you will be well equipped for most circumstances in daily life.

Most of us at the seminar had some experience with basic meditation, so we agreed readily when An-Shu mentioned the value of
the mental stability that can be gained through practice. I was first
introduced to meditation when I was just seven years old, and so I
had used it through most of my life to relax or modulate emotions.
In my To-Shin Do training, I was introduced to an even more pre-
cise form of meditation, to counter the tendency of the mind to get
distracted second by second. The ability to hold attention clearly
under pressure was critical to advanced martial practice.

These were what I usually thought of when reflecting on the
value of meditation. I was also aware of visualization practices
for calming, focusing, or goal-setting. However, I sensed that this
identification meditation might be something altogether new.
"An-Shu," I asked, "can you say more about directing the mind to
a certain perspective? I don't think I've done that kind of meditation before." It seemed a bit abstract to me.

A Fudo Myo'o shrine in Japan. —*Photo by Andrew Willett*

"You can start by holding the visualization of an image that gives you a certain feeling. The image itself carries the feeling for you, so you have something solid to hold onto."

"So, for example, for Kuji One, the image of Fudo Myo'o?" I asked.

"Traditionally, that might be what some of our ancestors used," he agreed. "However, they grew up on stories of wrathful deities. Their legends were full of such imagery, so when the image of Fudo Myo'o is presented or brought to mind, they already have the right associations in place. Americans first impression of these Asian deities may be less helpful."

He presented the group a picture of Fudo Myo'o in traditional form. "This character is a bit intense. I remember when I saw some of these characters, my first thought was, 'Wow, in the religion I grew up under, flames, weapons, snarling teeth, and claws are kind of associated with the bad guy. This is actually the good guy?'" Several of us chuckled at the reference. "So it may not be helpful to just put this Asian image of indomitable resolute strength out for everyone to imagine.

"Instead, we might think, what would be our own culture's version of that kind of strength and commitment, mixed with some fierceness? What legendary figure do we all know, that brings a kind of intimidating power to his commitment to stopping evil? Someone who dresses in dark blues and blacks, perhaps?"

We pondered it for a moment before someone shouted it out. "Batman!"

We laughed at what we thought was a joke, but An-Shu Hayes took it seriously. "Yes! Batman! Our culture knows him well, and we call him the Dark Knight. How many of you know a little of Batman's story?"

Everyone put their hand up.

"How many of you have seen a Batman comic, movie, or show? How many of you have some sense of what Batman is all about, as opposed to Superman or Spiderman?" Hands were strong all around. "So if we said to you, 'What would Batman do in this situation?' how many of you think you could come up with something?"

We could all do it. I wanted to laugh at the absurdity of meditating to be like Batman, but I couldn't laugh because I suddenly
could see how it was the analog to my ninja ancestors meditating
on Fudo Myo'o.

"Now, that's not to say you should be like Batman necessarily,"
continued An-Shu Hayes. "Our culture these days has a way of
making anti-heroes, tormented characters with all kinds of psychological issues. The ancient traditions did not recommend that.
But as an image, as a method of visualizing the kind of strength we
intend to embody, it may help to use something that inspired us as
children, something where we know the stories and the victories,
and they are built right in to that image for us."

Exercise Nine – **Identifying Your Hero**

Write down answers to the following questions and see what you
come up with.

1. When you think of immovable strength, who comes to mind
    first? It doesn't have to be a perfect fit, but see who comes
    to mind first. Write that name down.
2. Thinking of movies, books, and comics, what characters
    strike you as related to this idea of immovable strength?
    Write those names down.
3. Thinking of historical figures that you've heard or read about,
    who comes to mind as embodying this ideal of immovable
    strength? Write those names down.
4. Thinking of your own family and friends, who most carries
    the strength in your immediate circle? Write those names
    down.
5. Thinking of people you work with, public figures you've
    met, or friends-of-friends you have encountered, who
    have you met that seems to carry this ideal of immovable
    strength? Write those names down.

Now, of all these fictional, historical, and real-life characters, who among them is willing to take action to make the world a better place? Who among them carries a fierceness of making things happen? Identify those names.

Also, of all those characters, whose strength could you admire? Whose strength would you like to have, if it were possible?

For this exercise, select one character you have never met (a historical or fictional person) and one character you have met (a real person). Now it's time to generate details.

Write down the answers to the following questions about the historical or fictional person:
  • What clothes do they wear?
  • What gear do they always carry with them?
  • Where do they live?
  • How do they get around from place to place?
  • How are they known by others? How do people recognize them, and what do they think of them?
  • Are there any archetypal words or sounds this character makes?

Next write down the answers to the following questions about the real person:
  • When have you seen them embody their strength in its best form?
  • How did they speak, if at all?
  • How did they move, if at all?
  • What did they do, if anything?
  • What made it such a powerful response?

"It's important to be detailed about your visualization," An-Shu continued. "This is no mere hoping. The point is to bring to life, in your mind, the embodiment of the power you seek. The more real you make it in your mind, the more it is real to your mind. Let me ask, is anyone here a neuroscientist?"

One person in the group actually did raise their hand. An-Shu Hayes has always attracted a wide variety of powerful and successful people.

"Great!" An-Shu was totally unsurprised to have an actual neuroscientist in attendance. "So, keep me honest here. I have heard that brain scans have shown that imagining something in enough detail and experiencing it for real look the same inside the brain. Is that right?"

"Yes," the neuroscientist agreed. "In theory, imagining something with enough detail is indistinguishable from actually experiencing it. The same lessons are learned and memories are formed."

"Imagine that!" An-Shu said in a mock surprised voice. We all laughed at the double-meaning. Then his tone shifted down to a serious pitch. "This is really, really important. Think about it. I have only so much control over my external experiences. I might be temporarily out of contact with what I need for inspiration, learning, and growth. But if I have trained my mind to visualize well, I have access to that inner reality. I can go back to the experiences I need to have."

He paused for a moment to let that sink in. I started to wonder what experiences I needed to have, and he picked up my thought immediately. "What you need are experiences that reinforce in you your own access to the power you seek. The power is in there. You just need to remember that it's in there. You need to remember what it feels like to access it. And so, the method is to visualize coming into contact with that power in the form of this special person or being who embodies it. We visualize meeting that being, and that reminds us of what that power is like."

He gestured back to the image of Fudo Myo'o. "The details are important! The details bring the experience to life. In the ancient lore of our ninja ancestors, each detail of this character's

Fudo Myo'o statue in a Japanese temple. —*Photo by Justin Lowe*

clothes, weapons, and posture has meaning. Even his blue skin has meaning."

He proceeded to explain some of the lore. Fudo Myo'o (不動明王) in Japanese, or Acalanatha in Sanskrit, is one of the vidyaraja ("wisdom kings"), a whole collection of wrathful characters whose fierceness is devoted to protecting goodness and helping all beings cut through to truth. Fudo Myo'o uses his power to burn through confusion and compel attention to what needs to be done.

He carries a special flaming sword, with a vajra on the handle. The vajra is the symbol of ultimate truth in manifest form, and the flaming sword with a vajra handle is the ideal of cutting through delusion and confusion to get at the truth. Fudo Myo'o also carries a rope lariat, for restraining negative or distracting energies.

"Whatever creepy, wiggling negative energies might be hiding out in the shadows, Fudo Myo'o comes in with his intensity and his flame and lights them up. They try to run away, but he restrains them with his lariat. They try to fight, and he cuts them down with his sword. There is no space for that kind of negativity to hide, run away, or fight when he is around."

"An-Shu," I asked, "is Fudo Myo'o a warrior god then? Is he associated at all with martial arts?"

"It's easy to make that connection," he replied, "and a lot of warriors have followed Fudo Myo'o as an ideal. But he is not a god of fighting. He is a wisdom king, a master of wisdom who will not stand for foolishness, doubt, or confusion. He is so devoted to helping all beings break through to wisdom that he'll be tough on them if necessary."

"So, what about doubt or fear in oneself?" I asked.

"Yes. That is what it means. He'll go after those forces in you, with fire, sword, and rope if necessary. His inspiration is to cast out all doubt, fear, confusion, and distraction. When you imagine Fudo Myo'o, or whatever heroic figure of strength you choose, you are choosing to set aside those divisions in yourself that may incline you to give up. In the language of our own culture, you get fired up. You remember why it's important that you win, the people that are counting on you, and you set aside your own doubts to manifest the strength needed."

The room went silent for a moment. I was afraid to ask my next question, but I forced it out of myself. "So, just by imagining this character, all this will happen? Doubt and fear will go away?"

"It might be a little more involved than that," he answered. "Perhaps eventually, after a lot of practice, you could just bring your power image to mind and just like that, you'd be in the perfect state of mind. But to get there, you'll need practice, just like with the mudra and the mantra. You have to invest in the image."

"How do I do that?"

"That's what teachers are for, someone who has had the experience and can walk you through it skillfully. Luckily, that's why we are all here today."

 Exercise Ten – **Meeting Your Hero**

You really do need a teacher to take you through the depth exercise that An-Shu took us through that day. The teacher not only needs the experience and the proper perspective, but the skill to know just when to talk and when to go silent, just what to share directly and what to only suggest and let it arise from within. Such a teacher is extremely rare, but if it's important to you, you will find a way to spend time with one, just as those on the path before you did.

In the meantime, you can develop your skills. You'll get benefit from these exercises even if you never find a personal teacher. If you do find a teacher, you'll be more ready to engage what they can offer. Here's one way to build your visualization skill.

Find a place of solitude where you can take time to go into your visualization. It could be an inspirational place, but if you have a hectic life, it could be as simple as locking yourself in the bathroom for a few minutes of alone time.

Bring to mind some small topic or issue where you feel stuck or confused. The best topic for initial practice is something relatively trivial, some little side project where you aren't sure how to move forward. With such a minor topic, you can feel bold in your mental exploration.

If you completed Exercise Nine, you have developed a mental image of a personal heroic character, drawn from fiction or history. Now it's time to develop a conversation with that character in your mind. Where would that character likely be found? Do they have a base, an office, or a secret hideout? Or would they be found outdoors, on a battlefield or a mountain summit? Imagine where you would have to go to meet this character.

Let your eyes close so you can really go there. What would the journey be like? Perhaps you'd need some kind of time machine or inter-dimensional portal to go there. This is all in your imagination, so you get to create the details.

Take yourself through the journey in as much detail as possible. Find your personal hero, and approach them. They will be glad to see you and welcome you to their place of power. How does this powerful force acknowledge your arrival in a positive way? What gifts might you bring to this hero, to acknowledge them and ask for their help?

The powerful hero is interested in you and wants to help you. Once you have arrived in their place of power, acknowledged them and been acknowledged by them, ask them about your question or project. What advice would they have? How would they work with your problem?

Be ready for an unusual answer! Heroic beings give big answers, and their first answer may be metaphorical. You are not meant to follow their answer literally. It's an inspiration or an idea of one possibility. The hero gives you a perspective of how they would solve your problem. Then it's up to you to translate that into something effective and appropriate in your life.

Sometimes the hero really does show up.

My wife was out driving on a country road when she blew a tire. She pulled over, got out the spare and the jack, and attempted to loosen the lug nuts on the flat tire. Try as she might, however, she couldn't get the tire iron to turn. The lug nuts had been put on by a pneumatic wrench at a professional garage and they were too tight for her strength.

There was no one around on this abandoned road, no houses nearby, and no passing cars. It was before the time of ubiquitous cellphones. She knew she was going to have to work it out on her own.

She did the Kuji One mudra and the mantra, summoned up her inner strength, and strained with all her might, but she still couldn't get the wrench to budge. Feeling frustrated, she channeled that irritation into more focus on the mudra and mantra, building up her power. She was not going to quit. She imagined the power of Fudo Myo'o and visualized him standing nearby, sending his power into her.

Suddenly she heard footsteps behind her in the woods. She spun around to see a tall, broad man—rippling with muscle and purpose—step out of the woods, in a blue T-shirt that echoed the blue skin of the Japanese deity. He matched the physical and social presence of a god of strength.

"Hey there," he said amiably. "Looks like you're having trouble. Would you like me to change that tire for you?"

She simply nodded. He easily turned the lug nuts, jacked up the car, mounted the spare tire, and had her ready to go in a few minutes. He never asked for anything, but wished her a good day and walked back into the empty woods, where he faded into the wilderness.

CHAPTER 7

Becoming Strength

Boulder, CO, May 2008: After months of logistical planning, the day had come for me to lead my security team for the first-ever visit to Boulder of His Holiness the 17th Karmapa. I had divided the floor plan of the castle-like building into three strategic zones headed by my most trusted team members, my wife and two senior students from my dojo.

Zone One was the front of the house, led by my talented and powerful wife Mary. She needed to oversee the lobby and merchandise areas, the vendors, and the special VIP entrance where dignitaries of all sorts would be arriving and needed to be escorted to a VIP lounge before being taken to their balcony seating. She would need to find the balance between maintaining order in the face of a very entitled clientele and providing the high-touch service and diplomacy that the hosts wanted to present. If there was going to be a social or diplomatic problem related to power and money, Mary was going to be the first to manage it.

Zone Two included the public seating area in the main venue, as well as the exterior perimeter of the building. This zone was all about effective crowd management, and included numerous back-up plans in case of emergency evacuation. My trusted friend and student Jeff would leverage his Marine Corps experience to manage an enormous group of volunteer security guards, plus interface with local police and a private weapons-screening contractor team. If there was going to be a demonstration, public health issue, or logistical breakdown, Jeff was going to be the first to tackle it.

Zone Three was the high-security backstage area, underground infrastructure, tunnels, and catwalks. This zone had the highest level of control but also the most potential for sudden danger to arise with minimal backup because of the hidden areas. My longtime friend and brilliant student Thomas was in charge of conceiving every possible angle for covert activities and devising countermeasures and strategies for detection and containment. If there was going to be an attempt at theft, assault, or intrusion, Thomas was going to be in charge of responding.

Though we had spent much of the last several days at the site preparing, we arrived before dawn on the day of the event and made a last sweep of our own before the bomb-sniffing dogs came through. Satisfied that no one had hid in the building overnight, we let the dogs do their work while we assembled our teams outside. I met with the weapons-screening contractors to establish the details of positions and interaction protocols.

Immediately things started to go wrong. People were already starting to stand in line, and the weapons screeners weren't set up. The ushers for the event didn't know how to get through weapons screening, so they couldn't go in to set up. I was technically not in charge of the weapons screeners, but I involved myself before the whole situation collapsed.

"Listen," said the grossly obese security bureaucrat from the screening company, "I don't know who you are, but they told me no one goes in without screening and screening starts at 8 AM."

"Right," I said, "but this is the security team and the ushers for the venue. They need to get access now, so either screen them or take my word for it that they are clean."

"That's not what they told me."

"What who told you? Have you talked to Doug or Mark?" I was

referencing the men that I worked for, who were overseeing the whole Karmapa visit through multiple venues.

"What they told me down at the office," he said, waving a contract he held in his hand. He quickly put it away so I couldn't see what was written on it.

I realized that this guy was just following a set of automatic corporate rules from his boss. His boss probably didn't talk to my bosses either, but got it from the sales department at the security company. Communication breakdown.

"Okay, so here's the deal," I said. "I'm the one who has done all the logistical planning for this venue. I know who is coming and when they are getting here. I also know all the people paying the bills and what they want. I can make them happy, which means your boss will be happy, if I can direct your guys. I've also established a command center in the basement with refreshments, which you are more than welcome to enjoy while I make sure everything is working here."

He wasn't totally convinced, but at that moment I saw the police commander assigned to the event walking by in full uniform. We had worked together with the State Department officials during an earlier planning phase. I waved him over. "Are you guys all set up? Do you need any support from us?" I asked him. I knew he didn't need anything from us, and probably wouldn't take it if he did, but I was validating my own importance in front of the weapons-screening contractor.

"We're all set," the commander replied. "Just get out of our way if you see us moving. Otherwise, it's your show." He knew what was going on and had no particular love for the contracting company.

"Alright," the screening boss acknowledged. "Tell 'em what you need, and tell 'em I said to do it. If anyone gives you any lip, call me and I'll straighten 'em out." He lurched to his feet and wandered off toward the command center with the refreshments.

The power play was radically out of character for me. I'm the nice guy who doesn't want to upset anyone. Standing up in the presence of police and security forces was way outside my normal personality, but I knew I stood for something here. It wasn't for me that I needed to be strong. Literally thousands of people were coming today for a sacred experience, and it was my job to create a safe and functional space for that experience. I took that as my own sacred duty—sacred enough that I was willing to be some-body other than my normal self and play the tough guy. I was going to get this done.

I took control of the placement and protocols of the weapons-screeners. I let them do their jobs and use their expertise, but I told them when and where to do it so that the flow of people and events would go correctly. They were in Jeff's zone, so once I got our staff and the ushers in, I told him the plan and introduced him to the screeners so he could adjust them as needed.

Meanwhile, Mary was inside handling a diplomatic issue before any VIPs had even arrived. Our security team was mostly volun-teers who would be on their feet for about 14 hours, handling high stress people in a charged atmosphere. They would need energy and focus, so Mary had arranged for a spread of food in the com-mand center with fruit, vegetables, lunchmeats, bread, drinks, and more. The idea was that people could eat whatever they needed during their short ten minute rotation breaks and keep themselves sharp all day.

The trouble was, His Holiness the Karmapa was a proponent of vegetarianism and many of his spiritually minded American fol-lowers took that as law. As Mary was overseeing the food arrival, some of the people conducting morning prayers took offense at the lunchmeats and demanded that there be no meat at all in the building. With no sense of irony, these people rudely and violently demanded that the "dead animal meat" be removed so as to create a more pure spiritual atmosphere.

Mary was vegetarian for years at one point and respected the view. She also knew firsthand that it is very difficult for certain body types to stay healthy, especially while very active, on a veg-etarian diet. As team leader looking out for her people, she was well aware that some people should not be taken out of their normal food choices on a day of high physical and social stress.

She patiently explained to the angry ones that we had a large number of volunteers working security vigorously, and there was a whole range of body types, metabolic conditions, ages, and health levels. It would be inappropriate and even dangerous to force vegetarianism on them under such intense working conditions, without any knowledge of relevant health concerns.

They still insisted that it was a violation of the Karmapa's holy energy to allow meat in the building.

Mary was also a practicing Buddhist who was quite aware of the cultural issues. She knew that the historical Buddha was not a vegetarian, that Tibetans are typically not vegetarian, and that even His Holiness the Dalai Lama had taken to eating some meat on the advice of his doctor. She pointed out that the lunch tray would be in the secret command center in the basement, far away from the public or His Holiness. None of His Holiness' entourage or the general public would ever see it, smell it, or have contact with it in any way.

Still, the strident ones demanded that it be taken out of the castle-sized building immediately. They felt that the security staff, if they needed meat, should leave the venue, eat, and return. This of course was radically impractical given the very short shift rotations, the size of the facility, and the enormous security layers around the site that would take almost an hour to navigate in each direction.

Realizing what needed to be done, Mary nodded politely, personally took the lunch meat tray from the stunned and confused caterer, and proceeded toward the command center in the basement.

"What are you doing?" someone demanded. She ignored them and continued walking. "You can't do that!" they shouted. She ignored them and continued walking. She knew that some of her team members would rely on this protein to perform.

One of them ran up beside her and moved to physically block her way. She stepped around him. Finally, he reached out with a hand as if to restrain her or grab the tray.

Friends who witnessed told me later that her Kuji One energy went from subtle to overt. Her eyes blazed as she made eye contact with the objector. An exhale crossed her lips with the implication of a growl. She became solid and powerful. "Back. Off."

He gasped, flinched, and pulled his hand back as if bitten. He backpedaled. She walked away and no one objected further.

I arrived in the command center just in time to hear the story, as we set up the audio and video feeds for the security staff to take in the teachings while on break. Most of the security team were active meditators, many of them Buddhists, and so we set up a meditation area next to the feed so they could nourish their minds as well as bodies. It was important to me to take care of our team, so they could take care of the Karmapa, the hosts, the VIPs, and the general public.

I spent the next couple of hours sorting out minor glitches and communication issues as thousands of people arrived, were screened, and passed into the auditorium. Jeff was in charge of the exterior grounds, and his team caught and removed several people who tried to sneak into or hide in the area, presumably for photos or autograph demands. At last, it was time for the big moment of security choreography, when His Holiness arrived in caravan surrounded by entourage, private security, spiritual followers, State Department, police, and even a Secret Service agent acting as personal bodyguard. The vehicles flowed in smoothly just as we had planned, and the Karmapa and personal attendants emerged from SUVs and approached the backstage door under heavy guard.

A State Department agent was posted just outside that door, and Thomas and I waited just inside it. Thomas had negotiated an arrangement with the agent, so at the correct moment, he knocked on the door in just the right way, and we welcomed the entourage into the cleaned and secured stage area.

Thomas had spent the last couple of hours climbing ladders, checking catwalks for unauthorized persons, re-establishing security perimeters as local staff tried to break them, and engaging in dominance battles with the stage manager over the placement of personnel and equipment. He had handled it perfectly. Everything was in place, and he got an approving nod from me, the State Department agent, and the Karmapa's Tibetan personal head of security. His Holiness' presence filled up the backstage area and we experienced the thrill of being in arm's reach of such a powerful man.

The team swept in and the Secret Service agent led the way to the ready room where His Holiness would wait for a few moments before speaking. Once he was secured there, the agent emerged so she could take a short much-needed break before joining His Holiness onstage. We directed her to the restrooms and gave her a prepared badge with her name for our local security.

She returned shortly, the Karmapa emerged from the ready room, and the group went on-stage. The show began with great energy from the crowd. Thomas and I were enjoying watching from the wings when I got an urgent call on the radio from one of the police officers. He demanded to see me right away.

I scrambled through the secret passageways under the building to get to the front of the house quickly. I caught up with the officer and he pulled me aside so we could talk privately.

"We have a serious problem. This woman accompanying the Karmapa, she came through our checkpoint. When we asked for her ID, she flashed a CCW." He was referring to a permit to carry a concealed firearm. "I am required to arrest anyone who brings a firearm onto this campus, for any reason. Is she packing?"

"She's Secret Service," I replied. I had no idea whether she had a gun under her jacket, but it seemed likely. None of the rest of us had firearms due to the very restriction that the officer had referenced—the university campus was a strict no-firearms zone.

"Let me repeat. I am required to arrest anyone if I have reason to believe that they are carrying a firearm on this campus. I need you to tell me that you are going to resolve this and there is no reason to believe that she is carrying a firearm." I realized what was happening. He knew full well that she was Secret Service, and he knew that a massive scene would be caused if he tried to approach her and exert authority. He also knew that he was in a bad position because she might be violating laws he was sworn to uphold. He needed me to mediate.

"Sir," I said in my most formal voice, "there is no reason to believe she is carrying a firearm. I will speak with her and ensure that she is aware of campus policies."

He smiled. "Thank you. I consider the matter resolved." He nodded and walked away.

I wasn't sure how to move forward. There was no way that I was going to tell a Secret Service agent that she had to give up her gun. I didn't relish the idea of even broaching the topic of inter-agency cooperation with her, as she had already shown her disdain for the local police. Just trying to stop her for a conversation would probably cause a scene. Still, it was my job to see that this sacred experience did not collapse under the weight of politics and ego between the agencies that are supposed to make it safer. I summoned up my strength of spirit. This was not the time for overt strength, but I was going to need a good dose of bravery.

I got backstage, found Thomas, and updated him on the situation. "What are you going to do?" he asked.

"We're going to use the 'overhead information' trick," I replied. Thomas and I had discussed in the past that people are more likely to believe and less likely to take offense to information overheard than directly presented.

We waited until just before the first break in the talks. Thomas and I strategically positioned ourselves by the stairwell to the ready room. The entourage made their way off the stage, the Secret Service agent leading. We timed it perfectly. Just as she was entering earshot, I said to Thomas, "The local police are really concerned about weapons control. If any of your team is carrying, make sure they keep it quiet."

She broke stride just barely as I said it. I knew she processed it. She glanced at me and saw that I was looking at her, and in that moment, the whole story flashed between us silently. She paused very slightly, gave me a nod of acknowledgement, and continued on down the stairs leading her group. I had found a way to deliver the message.

Dayton, OH: "It's not for the sake of ego that we take on power," explained An-Shu. We were preparing to enter into the deepest of the meditations planned for the seminar weekend. "Fudo Myo'o is wrathful, but he is motivated for the good of all. His power cuts through confusion and restrains negativity."

I had heard this idea before, but it took on new depth after my experiences at the Karmapa event. The awareness of helping others, of facilitating something sacred, was so powerful at that event that it enabled me to rise above my own personality habits and take on power for the greater good. There was no question that it was not only pure because it was not ego-driven, but it was also far more powerful because I knew deep down the significance of my work.

I also knew that by keeping my eye firmly on the helpful contribution of my power, I was not seduced by power for its own sake. I could even enjoy my victories and moments of power, without fearing that I would become a petty dictator, because my whole fundamental reason for power was to help. The helping therefore not only empowered me but protected me.

"There is a phrase," An-Shu continued, "that absolute power corrupts absolutely. Have you heard that?" Many of us had. "But I don't agree. There was a time when I had absolute power over the lives of my baby daughters. How did I use that power? I used it to care for them, to make them stronger. They didn't always like it. Sometimes they fought me on it, but I used my power over them to help them. My love for them meant that my power was used correctly."

There it was: love and compassion as the forces that keep power on track.

"Do you think it's possible too," he continued, "that some of what you want and need for yourself would actually make the world a better place? Could you be an even better helper if you had more power, comfort, control, and peace for yourself? Of course you could. In fact, the world needs you to have those things, because the world needs your help in your best and most capable form."

 Exercise Eleven – **Dedication of Benefit**

What do you need or want? Write down three to five things that you want for yourself right now. Pick things that are personal, like a new car, a vacation, better health insurance, or some new clothes (as opposed to grand ideals like world peace or a cure for cancer).

Why do you want those things? Maybe you would be healthier, happier, or safer if you had them. Next to each one write down how those things would help you and make you more capable.

What could you do for the world if you had those benefits? For each one, imagine, "If I were happier, I could..." "If I were healthier, I could..." "If I were safer, I could..." Perhaps you could be more generous. Perhaps you could be less distracted and more available. Perhaps it would be easier to be kind. How would the world benefit if you had what you want?

Example:
I want more free time, a new car, and a bigger house.
More free time would let me feel more space in my schedule and give me more time to think.
A new car would give me the freedom to be where I need to be, when I need to be there.
A bigger house would give me a quiet room far from the daily action.
If I had more free time, I could clarify my ideas more and share them more skillfully in my writing and teaching.
If I had the freedom to be where I need to be, I could show up to more of my friends' special events and support them.
If I had a quiet room away from the action, I could focus better and be more productive when I am working.
Therefore, the world needs me to have more free time, a new car, and a bigger house. We all benefit.

An-Shu settled on his meditation cushion before us. "The ultimate form of this Kuji One training is that we become the heroic figure of strength. We walk in the world as that power. We don't start there because we have to clear away all these self-doubts. We may not really believe that we are capable of being that strong, so we have to verify it through action training, learning to say special words of strength, and tapping into our own imagination."

"We may also be afraid of that power. Can anyone believe that? That a person might be afraid of their own power?" Several of us nodded. "Why do you think someone might have that fear?" he asked.

"We might associate it with memories of abuse of power," I said.

"Or we might be worried about becoming arrogant," said another student.

"With power comes responsibility," said a third. "What if I use my power incorrectly and make a terrible mistake?"

"Right," nodded An-Shu. "All those things, and more. So we approach power gradually and verify as we go. We check it out and make sure we're okay, make sure our motives are pure, and reinforce positive, intelligent, and responsible uses of power."

I thought of the Code of Mindful Action that we say at the beginning of each To-Shin Do class. The Code is a series of ethical statements promoting the positive and reminding us to avoid the negative in 14 very specific ways. There is room in each statement for each individual to interpret how it applies to their life, and yet continuously reciting the Code reminds us that regardless of interpretation, there is a right way to live and use power responsibly.

Quest Center Code of Mindful Action

The first 2 points deal with material considerations.
I protect life and health. I avoid violence whenever possible.
I respect the property and space of all. I avoid taking what has not been offered.
The next 3 points remind you to be true to yourself.
I develop significant relationships. I avoid abusing others for selfish gain.
I thoughtfully express the truth. I avoid the confusion of dishonest words.
I cultivate a positive attitude, a healthy body, and a clear mind. I avoid whatever would reduce my physical or mental well-being.

The next 3 points guide communication with others.

I communicate health, happiness, and peace of mind to everyone I meet.
I avoid violent, disturbing, and unduly critical speech.

I promote harmony and positive momentum to bring out the best in everyone.
I avoid causing alienation, doubt, and division among others.

I encourage all to speak purposefully from the heart.
I avoid the dull contentment of gossip and small talk.

The next 3 points are keys for operating effectively in the world.

I am as enthusiastic about others' fulfillment as I am about my own.
I avoid treating others' successes as the cause of my lacks.

I promote the enjoyment of life, and encourage others with my smile.
I avoid setting myself against the world.

I strive for the personal realization of truth.
I avoid the seductive comforts of narrow-mindedness.

The final 3 points suggest how to generate accomplishment.

I accomplish what must be done in a timely and effective way.
I avoid putting off doing that which will benefit me and my world today.

I strive to be so strong that nothing can disturb my peace of mind.
I avoid the negative effects of worry, doubt, and regret.

I work to build love, happiness, and loyalty among all members of my family.
I avoid putting temporary personal benefit ahead of the welfare of those I love.

"And then, when we're ready, we can step into that power and just be it," he concluded.

"How do I know when I'm ready?" I asked immediately. I was looking for a feeling of surety before making the leap.

He smiled. "You try it out. You practice."

It struck me that it really was that simple. If I tried to practice and fell back from it out of fear, then I would know I had more homework and preparation to do. If I practiced and it kind of worked, I would know to just keep practicing. I realized that eventually I would just forget that I was practicing anymore—it would just become my natural way of being. At that point, I would have become it. Once again, An-Shu was able to cut through my emotions on the topic and help me see the direct nature of the path.

 Exercise Twelve – Walking as the Hero

An-Shu took us through depth exercises intended to wake up and recognize the inner hero in all of us. Again, a skilled teacher is really needed to arouse that heroic energy in just the right way, to let it come to the surface as a powerful feeling that restrains confusion and cuts through delusion.

That said, you might find that under the right circumstances, you can bring that mood to the fore on your own. Maybe somehow the music, the weather, the company, or the time in your life, brings you to that place where you feel like the hero that you studied and imagined before. You may find that you are no longer talking to the hero—you have actually become the hero for a moment.

If you are blessed to feel that arising, take advantage of it as a moment of practice. Do not doubt. It is not silly. It is not fantasy. It is identity meditation practice, just as it was when you were a kid and found real truths about who you could be during imaginary playtime.

You can indeed walk through life as a hero embodying strength. The more you have studied specific heroes of strength in your mind, the more possible it is that your mind will slip into that mood and help you feel that way. If you know the mudra hand-posture or the mantra words of Kuji One, you can lock in the feeling by taking the shape and saying the sounds. Record this memory of strength for later use.

Walk in it. Use it. Test it. Practice.

This Exercise Twelve happens spontaneously. Your job is to recognize it when you have an opportunity. Study what makes it true. Learn what takes you there.

And find a teacher if you can. Though authentic ones are extremely rare, they can help you find that feeling and understand what unlocks it.

2011, Boulder, CO: "What if I get lost in there?" my friend and student asked me.

We had been working on depth meditation exercises for identifying with the possibility of a larger and stronger self. In meditation, we temporarily let go of memories of being weak, small, and trapped. We imagined a self that was boundlessly powerful and ready to make the world a better place.

"In what way could you get lost?" I asked her.

She closed her eyes to bring words to her feeling. "There was a moment where I felt powerful and free. I wasn't worried about anything. But, some of things I worry about, I feel like they are good worries. I worry about them because they need doing, or they are things that need protecting."

Although I knew some things she worried about really could be released and forgotten, I acknowledged that some concerns are important and part of good projects.

"So what if I forget those while I'm off being powerful and free? What if I never come back?" she asked.

It was a good question, not because the threat is real, but because the fear is real. In my experience, those nagging doubts hold us back from our power and freedom. We feel like we would

The Shaku-Jo mystic's staff carried by explorers of the path.

be letting things collapse or letting people down if we really release those burdens, even for a moment in the privacy of our own meditation. And, just like my friend, I too had worried that I might not remember important things later, so I needed to hold onto them even when trying to build a new self.

"What I have found," I began carefully, "is that the important and necessary things come back to mind. The ones that fall out of our mind and never return can only do so because they had no role in our new life."

Some of my friends have a trick to prune down their material possessions when they feel they've gotten overburdened. They take all the things that they use rarely or never and place them in storage for 6 months. If in 6 months, they never think of the thing or wish they still had it, they get rid of it permanently. "It's like that," I shared, "except now we are talking about mental habits. A certain mental habit or line of thought might have served you once. It might have helped create a safe space or a rule of thumb while you were younger and developing in other areas. But now, you'll want to ask yourself whether those mental habits are still important. Some are, of course, and those ones will naturally come back to you when your powerful and free self returns to the world. Others are leftover from another time, and they can fall away."

I borrowed a metaphor from my teacher, on the rules of crossing a road on foot. As a young child, the rule is, "Never cross the road without holding a parent's hand." As time goes on, that rule becomes unsuitable. The child gains independence and the ability to observe and decide, and the parent is not always immediately at hand, so the rule changes to "Always look both ways before crossing the road."

However, even that good rule shifts with adulthood. Adults in their own quiet neighborhood probably don't stop and look both ways before crossing the street, because they know the rhythms of their local road so well that they know they have other ways of knowing whether a car is near. They can hear it, or see the reflections in certain surfaces.

Adults could not function if they needed their parents' hand to cross the road, and although they could function methodically looking both ways at every road, it would be odd and awkward. It is time for them to be more aware and free.

That said, an adult crossing an unfamiliar road in a foreign country had better stop and look both ways. An adult crossing a raging whitewater river may even take the hand of an experienced guide. The old lessons are still in there, but they are adapted to suit the expanded capabilities of the mature person.

"So it is with worry, self-doubt, and stopping to check to see if I am okay. In the beginning, we need to stop and check a lot because we have little experience and few instincts. As experience grows, we realize two powers that can give us more freedom from doubt. The first power is that we will know sooner when something is going wrong. We may forget to turn off the stove, but if we are aware, we will smell something burning soon enough to respond before the whole house catches fire. The second power is that we are more powerful—we can fix bigger problems, faster, because we are more powerful. Knowing that, we are free to focus on bigger tasks and truths. We can release the constant monitoring of the details."

"That makes sense. But what if I'm in there changing my identity, what if I forget something really big?" she asked. "What if I forget who I love, for example?"

"Do you know anyone that has happened to?" I asked.

"No, I don't think so. Well, maybe my grandmother in the final stages of Alzheimer's."

"Sure, with enough medical damage that can happen. But from meditation? From thinking?" I asked.

"No."

"Have you ever seen a documentary about such a case on television? Read a book about a case like that?" I pressed.

"No."

"Okay. So it's a very theoretical worry. We don't actually have history to prove that it could happen, unlike say a shark attack or a lightning strike."

"I guess that's true. But I still worry about it, and it keeps me from going deeper into the meditation."

"Yes. So you need to know that you can't lose something important to you. Here's how you can know that—the important thing became important to you once before. If it is still important, it will arise that way again."

There was a story once about a brain-damaged man whose conscious memory was only about 24 hours deep. He retained his skills and unconscious things like that, but each day he woke with no memory of who he was or where he was. His wife tended to him, and though she conceded that it was hard to manage all the logistics and continuity of their life without him, there was one amazing benefit.

He fell in love with her anew each day. Every day, for twenty years, he woke up, discovered her, and was overjoyed to fall in love with her.

Why did it happen so consistently, even though he doesn't remember their history? Because the basic person he was fell in love with the basic person she was. It couldn't be lost, because he was not changing. The outcome is predictable, because thoughts and emotions are a by-product of who we are at a deeper level.

I shared the story with my student. "That's not to say that you might not come out of meditation and realize you don't love someone anymore. If you have changed, you may realize that. It may be time for that. But you won't forget and lose something that is important and right in your life. If it is who you are supposed to be, what you are supposed to be doing, it will arise anew, over and over again, no matter how many times you forget or get distracted."

CHAPTER 8

Negative Emotions

"I guess that makes sense," my friend said. "Maybe too it's that sometimes I'm upset by what I realize wants to change. It's kind of soul crushing."

I remembered so many times over the years where I left the trainings with my teacher not feeling at peace. Sometimes I was merely unsettled by what I had realized. Sometimes I was embarrassed once I realized how long I had been holding myself back. In a few cases, I was even enraged by the suggestions of my own heart and mind.

I nodded in sympathy with her. "Yes, you'll want to pace yourself. This training is not for the faint-hearted. We want this great strength and power, but it does release some things along the way. Although this is definitely not about psychology and therapy, there may be some therapy you need to do, depending on what comes up."

"It seems very psychological sometimes. How is it different from therapy?" she asked.

I remembered asking my own teacher the same question. "Therapy is about finding out why you feel a certain way. And sometimes a feeling is so strong and overwhelming, you need to get that answered before you can move on. But this practice is about the moving on. When we're ready, this practice invites us to let go of the things holding us back, to literally forget them, or relegate them to unimportant footnotes in our life."

"That seems hard to do," she commented.

"Very hard to do!" I exclaimed. "That's why it's so rare to accomplish these Kuji powers, why we call them magic. They're not really magic in the sense of being from another dimension or something like that, but they are magic in the sense that we've gone beyond the ordinary person's view. We tapped into a greater truth and embraced it. Not easy. But worth it."

"So what do I do when hard stuff comes up?"

"Take a break. Take a breath. Take a walk. See if you can let it ebb and release over time, so you're ready to move on. And if you can't let it go, then go resolve it —in therapy, in life, whatever you need to do. Resolve it so you can move on."

"But why does this stuff have to come up at all?" she asked.

"It's like snot coming out after a cold. We don't like having to blow our nose, but that's just the symptom of what's going on in our blood. Dealing with the symptom is an irritation, but the symptom actually means we're making progress. That snot is composed of the white blood cells and broken-down parts of the invading illness. It is the proof that our body is fighting the invasion, and getting closer to health. You may not like the emotions and insights that hit sometimes as you are unlocking your strength, but those emotions and views were already in you. Those bad feelings aren't coming from the practice—they are coming out because of the practice, and they are coming out so you can move on."

I paused before delivering my final advice. "Take your time. Only take on what you feel ready for. Avoid extreme actions and statements, especially when those feelings come on strong. But gradually, keep going. I can tell you from personal experience, it's worth it."

CHAPTER 9

Vajra Time

T he insight of the Kuji has a funny way of existing outside of time. Of course, the training experiences change you, so you will act differently and have new experiences in the future. However, they also change the meaning of your memories. You may come to realize that you did in fact experience this energy before, long before you ever trained in it, and you can recognize it now that you have practiced. In this way, the training actually reaches back through time, changing your past.

The memories of the energy also exist in a kind of virtual time, where five minutes one week could connect with three minutes of another week, plugging into a memory several years old and then empowering a future months hence. Because of this, you may realize a profound lesson in a moment wholly unremarkable to anyone else present, or the realization may not hit you until long after a significant moment has passed.

My teacher calls this Vajra Time—the time wrapped around the ultimate truth represented by the iron battle mace from ancient India and Nepal. The truth slams into you like a battle mace at times, and what was invisible a moment before cannot be unseen now.

2007, Boulder, CO: My longtime student Thomas was crossing a parking lot on a sheet of ice. He used his To-Shin Do ninja foot-work to glide carefully over the super-slick surface and keep his balance. His mission tonight was to get to the grocery store to get some medication for the flu he had, and then get home to bed without falling down.

He was quite ill and exhausted, and other pedestrians had already fallen nearby, so his attention was on walking carefully. Therefore, he didn't notice at first that the white van driving across the parking lot was going too fast for the icy conditions.

There was a stop sign and a crosswalk, but somehow he got a feeling that something was wrong. He stepped into the cross-walk but stopped short of the middle just as the van completely lost traction at the stop sign. The van slid forward at maybe ten miles per hour—slow for a vehicle, but still more than you want to be hit by as a pedestrian. Thomas had a moment of relief as he pulled up short, feeling smart that he listened to his intuition and stopped walking.

Then the van slid sideways as the driver attempted to swerve away from Thomas. The rear of the van swung out in a big sweep-ing arc. Thomas had only a second to respond, and he couldn't move quickly due to the ice. Adrenaline swept away the flu and his righteous indignation fired up. The strength power of Kuji One surged through him and he sent his energy deep down into the earth, rooting into his position right through the ice.

His hands came up, and as the van came into reach, he double palm-slammed the side panel. The impact boomed into the metal and the van ricocheted off of him, straightened out of the fishtail.

The van drifted further and finally coasted to a halt on the ice. The driver had heard the impact and tried to get out, but couldn't get enough footing on the ice to even walk around and check on Thomas. "Hey, buddy, oh man, are you okay?" he hol-lered, a bit panicked.

Thomas was still standing in the same spot, feet rooted in the ice, heart pounding. He was physically unharmed, but the energy was so strong in him that he couldn't form words yet. Breathing heavily, he glanced up at the van and saw two basketball-sized dents where his hands had struck it. The absurd thought crossed his mind that he might get in trouble for denting the vehicle. Then he realized how crazy it was going to be to explain how he used ninja magic to palm-strike a van away from him.

"I. Am. Fine." He managed to growl it out one word at a time. Drawing his energy back in, unsticking his feet, he willed himself to walk forward and away. The driver, relieved that he wouldn't have to account for running over a pedestrian, got back in the van and drove off as well.

"How did you know you could do it?" I asked Thomas later. "What made it seem reasonable to attack a car with your bare hands, when a moment before it was hard to even walk on the ice?"

"I had no choice," he replied. "I wasn't going to just let myself get run over."

Indeed. When you have eliminated the unacceptable, whatever remains, however incredible, must be your course of action. Spiritual strength is a refusal to accept helplessness.

Over the years of martial arts training, we started to notice a technique we came to call "ki shielding"—sending your energy to a certain part of your body to reinforce it before impact. It's not the same as tensing the muscles. Muscle tension actually makes the muscles hurt more if the impact goes through, and makes the body rigid and prone to breakage and strain. However, people tense their muscles instinctively because it does send their ki, their body energy, to that part of the body when they do it, and so the ki helps.

With practice, we learned to send our ki quickly to an area without having to tense the muscles. Therefore, we could be reinforced energetically and yet still responsive and relaxed in the force of the impact. The technique is just an extension of the same ki sending method we used in the Unbendable Arm exercise or anytime we project force, but in this case, we are simply reinforcing rather than projecting. It's easiest to send ki out the hands, because we are used to sending our intention to manipulate the world through our hands anyway. Then people learn to send it through their feet, elbows, and other striking surfaces. Finally, the ki shielding technique lets a person send their ki wherever it is needed, and in a split second as a defensive response.

I was cruising on my snowboard at about 25 mph, according to GPS records of the crash, when I got hemmed into a narrow track by two other skiers. No problem by itself, but then we all came around a corner, and a fourth person had stopped dead, right in my track. There was nowhere to go, and I realized this person who had stopped did not see me coming. We were both about to get very hurt.

I leapt into the air and attempted to jump over the downed person and into a safer line. I cleared him, but just barely, and I had to twist so much to miss him that I couldn't bring the board down flat out of the jump. My edge caught as I came down, and in that split second I felt my training kick in as time went into slow motion.

I knew I was going to get whipped into the ground, hard. My hands came up in a break-fall shape, and I sent ki into my arms. Boom! I bounced off the ground with my upper body, and my board took a violent left turn. I was passing a closed ski run at the time, and the turn rocketed me toward a sharp drop off marked off by thin steel poles and ropes. I was heading right for a pole.

I could see my default arc was for my neck to hit the pole. I tucked my chin so it would catch my helmet instead and sent ki to my skull.

The impact was loud, taking a gouge out of the helmet and trading paint with the steel pole. I was okay, but I went off the edge of the drop with enough remaining speed that I went airborne, rotating randomly from the impact.

My eyes couldn't orient visually with the speed, the spin, and the impact, so I pushed my ki out in all directions like radar to get a sense for where the next impact would be. I assumed it would be the ground, but a heartbeat before the slam, I sensed a tree coming up behind my right shoulder. My ki shifted to reinforce the shoulder.

Impact. Now spinning in the air in the different way. Definitely bruised, but no broken bones yet.

Now the ground. Reinforce. Impact.

Now sliding out of control, disoriented, in the woods. Another tree, reinforce, impact. I got a view of the woods as the last impact spun me again and my eyes could figure out up from down. I saw a sapling in my path and willed myself toward it. I bounced airborne again, but I was able to push off toward the sapling. I spread my ki wide across my body and hugged the softer tree.

It bent under the impact and my ki reinforcement held my body safe. I finally stopped, a few feet off the ground, and then slid down the soft branches to the ground. The whole crash was three seconds start to finish.

I was physically intact, but I couldn't move. The energy that had kept me safe was like a force-field holding my body, and I had used so much adrenaline and mental power to make all the physical and energetic gymnastics happen. I was completely still in the snow, heart pounding, heat pouring out of me. I could hear people calling me from somewhere up above, but I couldn't form words.

A few of the folks involved in the crash came down the closed run to find out if I needed medical attention, or perhaps the coroner. I let my breath out with a shudder, releasing some of the Kuji energy, so I could reply to them.

"I'm okay… where am I?"

They thought I had a concussion and named the resort.

"No, I know that, I'm just not sure what run I'm on, or how far down."

They laid it out for me. "Are you sure you're okay?" one guy asked. "That was a crazy crash."

"Yeah, I'm okay." I forced myself to my feet. I was going to need a few minutes to let the adrenaline cycle and get my legs back under me, but I really was okay. In fact, it was a great victory.

1995, Mt. St. Helens, WA: Mary and I brought six friends to explore the lava tubes under Mt. St. Helens. We had hiked through them a few months prior, taking about two hours to navigate the two mile underground tunnel that snaked up through the volcano to emerge halfway up the slopes.

Although the tunnel does not branch, it can be very uneven and twisty in places. It was formed when flowing lava carved a hole through the mountain, cooled at the edges, and then flowed out from the center, leaving a navigable passage that follows the unpredictable forces of an ancient volcanic eruption. Over the millennia since formation, parts have collapsed back into the tunnel, meaning that some areas are polished smooth from the original flow, and others are piles of shattered rock as big as a house inside of large underground chambers. Some areas are so big that you can barely make out the walls with your flashlight, and some are so small that you have to take off your pack and slide it ahead of you as you crawl.

There is a sense, as you move through the mountain, of exploring secret places inside the heart of the earth. It feels like there must be dwarves or goblins here, living hidden in this deep underground place. It's quite a wondrous journey, and we were excited to share it with our friends and my teenage sister. We drove up to the site thinking to begin the hike in the early afternoon, emerge from the tunnel high on the slopes in mid-afternoon, and hike back to the cars by dusk. We wore light jackets and jeans and brought just some water, thinking we would get dinner after the hike.

There is a darkness is caves rarely witnessed on the surface world. Normally, we think of darkness in terms of "too dark to make out details," but even in a dark house there are usually several light leaks from electronics or door edges. Outside, there is nearly always some ambient light. Even starlight is enough, once your eyes adjust, to make out general shapes that are within a few feet of you.

Cave dark is another matter. It is 100 percent pure darkness. You can wait as long as you like, but your eyes never adjust. Someone can wave their hand inches in front of your open eyes, and you have no idea. In the absence of even the suggestion of shapes, your brain starts to make up ideas about what might be out there. A creeping feeling of vulnerability can easily slip into a sense of dread, as your mind suggests that there might be vampires, cave bears, or serial killers hiding in the perfect black. You start to think that maybe you are seeing something, or hearing some subtle sound.

Then you turn the flashlight back on, spin in a circle wildly checking every direction, and laugh with your friends. That was the experience we wanted our friends to have.

We were college students, so we lacked the money to go to the store and buy gear. We had scrounged up used flashlights from various sources, and some extra batteries from other electronics. We had borrowed water bottles and put on our least worn-out shoes. We were ready for adventure.

When we arrived at the site, we discovered that the caves were seasonally closed. There was no fence or gate, just a sign announcing that the caves were no longer being patrolled or maintained until spring, six months away. We had just missed the official season by a day.

We debated, but we were excited for the adventure. "What's one day?" we reasoned. "Let's do it."

We descended into the lower entrance of the cave and began ascending the interior of the mountain. We stopped a couple of times in the first quarter mile to amuse our friends with the experience of cave darkness. Everyone was wildly uncomfortable with it, but when we made a circle with our backs to each other, we could turn off the flashlights for a couple of minutes and experience the phenomenal sensory deprivation of the silent underground.

We were about 40 minutes into the two hour hike when the first of the batteries started to dim on one of the flashlights. No big deal. We put in new batteries. The second flashlight began to dim shortly after. We put in more batteries.

A few more minutes of climbing, hiking, and scrambling over the broken subterranean landscape and the third flashlight suddenly quit completely. We couldn't get it to work again, but there were enough other flashlights that we could work around it with overlapping beams.

They say that if you boil a frog slowly, he doesn't realize that he should hop out of the water. I don't know if that's true, but now I do know that if you take away the light very gradually from a group of optimistic adventurers, they might not make the decision to turn back. One by one, flashlights failed or dimmed, yet we continued on our journey.

There came a decision and discussion moment more than an hour in to the hike. Only three flashlights were still functional. Our main storage site of extra batteries, in my friends' jacket, was revealed to be missing with the revelation, "Dude, there's a hole in my pocket...."

I remembered that it was a two hour hike with Mary and I, so I reasoned that however little light we had, at 75 minutes in, we would do better to go forward than back. Simple math that overlooked the psychology of pressing deeper into unknown darkness.

At 90 minutes in, we were down to one flashlight and a lighter as sources of light. In 1995, none of us had cellphones or anything else with a bright light-up LED screen. A lighter only makes light until it gets too hot and burns your fingers, forcing you to let it go. We mostly operated on the single flashlight from the back, awkwardly projecting a cone of dim light. As the beamholder swept the light across the cave, we each did our best to make out the twisted piles of rocks when the light touched them, and then navigate carefully from the memory of that brief and pale vision.

By two hours in the cave, we were in full darkness. The last of the light sources was exhausted, and we were truly blind. We had gotten used to it gradually, using touch and instinct more and more to move along. I was certain that we must be very close to the exit now, so I kept promising the group that Mary and I had done this before, that we were almost there. "Don't worry," I said, "We'll be fine. Just move carefully."

Another full hour passed like that, according to the one wristwatch we had with a tiny light-up face. We talked and sang, played Marco Polo in the dark, to keep our spirits up. There was a note of panic sometimes in the returning "Polo!" but it was critical to keep people talking. The only way we could know we hadn't lost someone was when their voice came to us.

At the three hour mark, however, the group stopped for a rest and started to lose it. It was only supposed to be two hours. "Why aren't we there yet?" someone asked.

"I... I don't know," I replied, "but we must be close. There is no way to actually get lost. It's a straight shot."

Mary leaned over and whispered to me. "We're not even to the crawling part, or the climbing part." She was referring to the section where we'd have to remove gear and push it, and the further section that actually required an eight foot vertical climb to access the next tunnel section.

"Weren't those near the end?" I whispered back.

"I thought they were like halfway," she said.

At some level, I thought she was right, but I realized everyone was listening to us despite our whispers. The cave was dead silent. There was nothing else to hear. "No," I said boldly, "I think we must have gone around those parts. We are close to the end."

"What if we really are lost? Didn't the sign say that no one would come through here for six months?" asked my sister.

Silence hung in the air. "Okay," I said carefully. "There's no point in thinking about that. I know we can't actually get lost. It's just a giant tube from one side to the other. We just have to go slow and stay safe."

"I think I'm bleeding," said one of my good friends who went by the name Zero.

"What? Where? Why?" I asked. I wanted to see the wound, but there was no way to do so.

"From my forehead. I walked into a rock a while back and broke my glasses on it," he replied casually.

I wanted to ask why he didn't say anything then, but then I realized that there would have been no point. Broken glasses don't mean much in darkness, and they probably fell into a crevasse after falling off his face.

"Me too," said another friend. "I think I tore my shin open." He paused. "A little."

I shook my head and rubbed my face in the darkness. It was so hard to read mood with no body language or posture to observe.

"Okay, let's make a plan," I said. "Zero, you lead the way by feel and describe what you are feeling as you go. That will warn us and also help us know where you are and which way you are going." I also knew that focusing on descriptions would keep all of us from thinking about survival issues. "I'll be right behind you." I wanted to keep touch with the middle of the group.

"I'll take the rear," said Mary. I knew I could count on her to make sure no one was left behind, and to call out if she needed help or a break. Some of the others seemed to be inclined to just fall down silently.

Everyone took the remainder of their water now, and we began to move slowly forward again.

I walked both my shin and my forehead into sharp rocks at some point. I would think I had an intuition for where the rocks and the space where, and then I would slam into merciless cold stone. Pain would arc through my body, and combined with the fatigue, fear, and frustration I would want to break down in tears for a few moments. I knew the others were having the same thing. We were trying to be strong, but I would occasionally hear suppressed sobbing from the people around me, and Mary's gentle comforting whisper.

I had to close my eyes while I moved. After hours of my irises straining to open just a little wider, struggling to get any light in at all, I could feel the muscles of the irises cramping inside my eyeballs. It gave me a headache to open my eyelids, so I had to close them. Irrationally, closed eyes made me feel like I couldn't move forward, like I was somehow more blind with my eyes closed. I fought my body instincts and forced myself forward, but then when I would hurt myself doing it, the idea was reinforced even more that I should just sit down and stop moving.

The worst was when we stopped for a break. We had to stop sometimes, as fatigue and now hunger were weakening us. We had to do a head count, tend to minor wounds, and boost spirits. Then it was enormously difficult to get the group moving again. We all just wanted to lay down and stop, even though we knew that led to nothing but death. I think some of us were literally willing to lay down and die, but I wasn't. Mary wasn't. Zero wasn't. The three of us took the role of group prodders, and we forced everyone back on their feet over and over, even though we deeply felt the temptation ourselves.

We checked the time and discovered that we were over four hours in now. It began to dawn on me that the group was moving much more slowly than Mary and I had when it was just the two of us. The darkness, the group dynamic, and the injuries were stretching the time out. I tried to estimate what that meant for comparison to our time, tried to estimate distance, but I couldn't build an intuition anymore.

The watch's glow-face was fading out from excessive usage for time checking and as a very weak light source to examine injuries. We wouldn't be able to check the time much more. I realized it didn't matter now anyway. The sun was setting about now, somewhere above us through hundreds of feet of rock, and we were committed to keep going to the end or die trying.

Not long after, Zero quietly called me forward while leading. I scrambled up to him, touched him to find his exact position, and leaned in for a private conversation. "What's up?"

"I can't find a way forward. It's dead-ended," he said.

"Are you sure?" I asked.

"I've been working this area for several minutes now, leading you guys around this cavern, but I can't find anything but the way we came."

I sighed. I felt like this couldn't be happening. I doubted my own memories now. Maybe the cave could branch? "Let me try myself," I said.

Zero pulled up the group for another rest break while I scouted. I took my time, feeling everything I could along the cavern walls, just hoping for a little edge that revealed the route. I found a crevasse leading deeper, but I knew that wasn't the route.

When I did find the way forward, I was relieved and disturbed at the same time. It was the crawlspace Mary had mentioned hours ago. Zero had missed it because the opening was only about two feet by two feet. It meant that we were just over halfway through the cave.

I had convinced myself that we had bypassed it somehow, found a way around it, even though that didn't make sense with my assertion that there was only one way through these tunnels. I just couldn't believe that it took us four hours to go halfway, when Mary and I had done the whole thing in two hours.

Privately, I grieved the fact that when we made the decision at 90 minutes to keep going, we were less than a fourth of the way in. It would have been far, far better to turn back then. It felt like we had come so far in these four hours. I knew it was only a two mile route, so we'd covered about a mile, but it felt like ten miles.

Now what? I wondered. *Do I tell them? Do we go back? Do we press on?*

I realized that spirits would collapse if they knew how much further it was going to be. We would not be able to get them to go on. At best, we'd have to divide the group, send scouts to get help, and try to rouse the rangers in the middle of the night to mount a rescue. At worst, the scouts would get lost or the group go into crisis at the division. I thought of all the horror movies where the characters say, "Let's split up to cover more ground," and then get picked off one by one, alone in the dark.

If I tell them that we are halfway, they will despair. It really is the same backwards and forwards now. If I tell them we should go back now, they will know exactly how far back it is, and they will have lost all faith in my leadership and judgment. It wasn't for my ego, but for their strength of spirit, that I decided not to clarify the situation.

I took a deep breath, calmed myself, and put on my best optimistic voice. "Good news, all! We've found a landmark. I know exactly where we are. We are on track. We're going to make it." I didn't dare step away from the crawlspace for fear of losing it in the dark. "Please join me over here."

The group slowly made their way to me. "Okay, so this is a little bit of a tricky section, but it can be fun," I said bravely. I remembered the panic the crawlspace induced in me when I did it the first time, fresh, relaxed, and with a flashlight. "We're just going to have to take off our packs, push them ahead of us, and crawl through this little section."

"Wait… it's so small that we have to take off our backpacks?" someone said.

"Yes, but it's not too far," I said.

"I'm not doing that," said another person. The words hung awkwardly in the air.

If you don't do it, you'll die down here, I thought, but said nothing.

"Kevin, are you sure this is right?" said Zero. He had put together the conversation Mary and I had earlier and knew what was going on. I could tell from his voice that he was not willing to lead the route into an unknown hole in the rock.

I could smell the fear from the group. I was losing them. We were all losing it. There was only one thing to do. "Okay, I'll lead the way!" I said brightly.

I was terrified too. *Am I really right? What if I fall into a hole and die? What if it collapses on me?* I tried to clear my mind of those thoughts, but I couldn't help but hear them. I knew that I had to move us forward, and I was certain that this was the route. *Besides, if I do die, then they'll know to turn back.*

I tied a rope to my backpack. I didn't want to push it ahead of me in the pitch black because I needed to feel the way. I tied the rope to the pack with plenty of leftover line on each side, so we could pull the bags through on the rope, pull the rope back, and thereby drag the bags through one at a time. It wasn't how Mary and I did it when we had light and focus, but it was what we needed now. If someone got stuck inside the crawlspace with their bag, we'd have no way of helping them or calming them, so I wanted to minimize complexities.

I took the rope, squatted down, and started crawling. The darkness seemed even darker in that hole, and the silence even more silent. I was divorced from the world, from the group waiting back there for me. I was totally alone and vulnerable, the stone touching me on all sides as I moved forward, and it felt like the entire volcano was pressing down on me. It seemed like it could swallow me up in a single moment, and the crawl itself went on three times as long as I remembered. I lost faith before the end and slowed way down, feeling each inch of ground to make sure I wouldn't fall into a pit or impale myself on sharp stone.

And then suddenly it opened up and I was in the cavern on the other side. I felt around carefully and stood up. Waves of joy and freedom moved through me for the first time on our dark journey. I had passed some kind of initiation moment, taken bravery and leadership to a new level.

The crawlspace was straight, as I remembered, so I called back that I'd made it and then pulled my bag through. They pulled the rope back and sent the rest of the bags, one by one. Even though I was in another cavern, alone, I didn't feel alone anymore. The stone was my ally. We could do this.

Once I had all the gear, people started coming through. They chose to use the rope too, a kind of familiar reassurance that they were on the right track. It was smart. A few of them arrived crying, but they made it. There were some long pauses between people, when Mary must have been convincing them to move forward.

Finally, Mary came through, bringing up the rear. We hadn't discussed who would be left behind in the last cavern, the terrifying crawl still ahead, but she had taken it upon herself to make sure no one was left behind. She too had that still moment, alone in the dark, and she arrived shaken but intact.

For all of us, it was a major turning point. We rested again, letting adrenaline and emotion ebb, but something had changed. We felt closer to the end than the beginning. We had successfully challenged the fear of the dark and the isolation, and now the pitch black caverns felt spacious and freeing in contrast to the crawlspace.

We went on for more time, unknown time now without reference point, and reached the next technical challenge. The eight foot vertical was easy to recognize since the tunnel narrows before it and terminates at it. It was hard to climb in the dark, feeling one's way to footholds and handholds, but no one panicked. It was a methodical process, and we surmounted it.

The next challenge was not the dark, but the light. We spotted the soft glow very early, eyes attuned to even the faintest emanation. We could see it around the corner of the tunnel, see the edges of rock in a way that we hadn't for hours before. I turned that corner to find Zero standing in what looked to be a beam of radiance from above.

The cavern roof had collapsed, and the open starry sky was revealed above. There was no moon, but the starlight was like daylight for us. At this high altitude deep in the wilderness, the stars were diamond-hard in the sky. It looked like another dimension, a portal straight from the underworld to the heavens, bypassing the mortal realm.

Alas, it was not the exit. It was merely a skylight in a cavern, some sixty feet above us. The way forward was a return to the all-consuming darkness as the tunnel continued out the other side. Zero was eyeing the impossible vertical pitch of the cavern walls.

"You'll never make it," Mary whispered as she and the rest of the group glided into the starlight, awestruck.

"But what if I could?" whispered Zero back. She physically put her hand on his arm to restrain him from attempting the lethal climb.

We could see each other for the first time in hours. We wiped dusty tear-streaked faces, scraped off dried blood from wounds. We smiled and cried a little. We were so hungry, so cold, and so beaten by the journey, but at last here was a reminder that we were among real people, and the outside world still existed.

We glanced warily at the black continuance of the tunnel. We knew we had to do it. We dreaded it, but we were no longer afraid of it. The return to the darkness took fortitude, but somehow the starlight had refueled our souls. We knew what to do now, and we had accepted our situation.

Time blurred after that. The tunnel features were simple, and our established rhythm of moving and talking carried us along. We were out of our bodies and out of our minds with fatigue, just repeating the pattern, past emotion.

I spotted the subtle glow of the exit at last. It was far dimmer than the starlight shaft, because the exit was a ladder in the middle of a cavern, leading to a manhole-sized opening drilled several feet through the cavern roof. My body shook as relief washed over me in waves.

"This is it!" I announced. "We made it!"

I immediately started up the ladder as the rest of the group gathered at the base. I scrambled up to the top and gasped when the cold air hit me. The top of the ladder led to a field that I remembered as warm and filled with wildflowers. Instead, I found six inches of snow on frozen ground, and a cold wind under the hard stars. My watch, visible in the moonlight now, said 11:30 PM. We had spent over 8 hours in the cave.

We were not dressed for this level of cold. Although it was only a two mile hike to the car, I knew we would suffer. I also couldn't spot the trail down. Last summer, it had been visible as a worn footpath through the vegetation, but now the snowy pine forest was trackless.

One by one my friends popped up out of the exit, like giant prairie dogs emerging from slumber. They blinked their eyes at the space and the moonlight, transfixed by the beauty, stunned by the cold, and thoroughly disoriented.

By the time Mary emerged from the ladder, discussions and complaints about the cold had already begun. "Well, we could spend the night in the cave for warmth," she said. Everyone's eyes narrowed. A palpable sense emerged that we'd rather die in the cold than re-enter the dark prison.

"I think we need to get moving," I said. I was the navigator. I needed to make a call.

I took a deep breath, turned toward the forested downslope so they couldn't see my face, and closed my eyes with a little prayer. *I need help here. I need to find the way down, right now.* I didn't know to whom the prayer was directed, as I was not particularly religious, but now was the time for divine intervention.

A wolf howled in the forest below us.

My jaw dropped open. *Seriously? Wolves?* I thought. *The blindness, the cave, the snow wasn't enough? Now wolves?*

The wolf howled again, and another one joined him somewhat further down the mountain. I heard their voices clearly on the wind, and the space between them mapped out in my mind. I saw a line between their voices, snaking down the mountain.

Suddenly I got it. The wolves weren't there to eat us. They were showing me the way.

A part of me doubted it. Was I just going crazy now under the pressure? But what choice did I have? I needed to lead these people to safety, and time was precious as the cold sapped our weakened bodies. The line was clear in my mind.

"This way!" I said boldly and started toward the invisible line in the forest that was painted in my mind by the howls. No one else seemed to have made note of the howling, which I figured was just as well.

The group shuffled along behind me, tennis shoes letting snow into socks. We wound our way down through the woods, and I kept thinking we would find the trail I remembered, but it never seemed to emerge. This was like an entirely new place, and yet we were sheltered from the wind and heading in the correct general direction.

Then the trail terminated at a steep slope that dropped hundreds of feet into a stream below. I was a bit ahead of the group, and I stopped suddenly at the surprise view. Frustration arose. *How can this be?* I thought. I approached the edge, looked down. There seemed to be no reasonable way forward.

The wolf's voice howled again, close this time. There was a big boulder just a couple feet down the precarious pitch, and the howl seemed to come from just behind it. I couldn't figure out how there could be anywhere there for a wolf to stand and howl.

"Okay, hold up. Let me just make sure this is the way," I said to the group before they got close enough to see the edge. No one replied, but they stopped.

I hopped down to the boulder and looked to the left, where the sound had come from. There was no wolf, but a secret trail carved into the side of the slope. I could see that it ran down the valley in the same direction we intended to go, but because of its position next to steep terrain, the wind had carried the snow past it. It had been sheltered from the snowfall and was completely dry.

"Here it is!" I said cheerfully as if I knew that all along. *Thank you,* I said in my mind to the invisible wolves and whoever was behind them. The trail led us gracefully down, without wind or snow. We reached the cars relatively intact, miraculously, well after midnight and took solace in the sanctuary of the heaters and the headlights.

It struck me that at the end of the day, everyone had carried themselves through that cave and down the mountain. Though we supported each other, no one collapsed and had to be rescued. Strength of spirit overcame enormous physical and mental challenges. We never gave up, even when the way forward was hidden from us. Although I did not know of Fudo Myo'o or Kuji One by those names, the spirit of strength was in every one of us. It was a part of our human birthright, activated by the right people in the right place and time.

February 2010, Boulder, CO: I was 11 miles in to a 14 mile wilderness run. I had worked all day and hit the trail at 11 PM. Ice and snow covered the ground and the night was pitch dark. It was ridiculous, but I was feeling strong and loving the feeling.

I like to run in the dark, with just enough light to stay on trail. It fires up my senses and make me feel even more connected. I make mistakes and crash sometimes, but when it goes well, I feel a heroic inner self come to the surface.

I had heard animals running alongside me earlier. I had listened to the wind roaring through the trees around me. I had felt all manner of wild energies stirring in the dark as I passed by, and I felt like an elemental force instead of a human being.

I was surprised to see a blue light in the distance. Who else would be out here at this hour, deep in the cold wilderness? I had run this trail in daylight and seen only a couple of people. I fully expected to be alone now. I felt mild disappointment that I could not be alone even in this most wild of places.

The blue light bobbed erratically toward me as I ran, and I got the sense of another runner. *Okay,* I thought, *here's someone who is just as tough and crazy as me. I have to salute that. We will pass for just a moment, two fellow adventurers.*

The light drew closer, and I could see that it was indeed another runner. However, he did not look at all as I would have expected. Instead of a lean runner's frame, he had a stocky, powerful body. His legs were particularly massive.

He was dressed all in blue, and carried some kind of rope. The blue light came from his forehead, where I supposed he had a headlamp. He looked a bit grouchy, a bit fierce.

As we got close enough that some kind of social contact was mandatory, I made eye contact with him. The trail was narrow, but it was dark and hard to see his face. It was when his mouth split into an ugly, toothy grin that it struck me who I had encountered on the trail.

He bowed his head in a wordless acknowledgment as we passed. He was just as tough and crazy as I, or I as he. In the split moment of the passing, I saw Fudo. He disappeared into the darkness and my memories, but I remembered.

What is really real?

After things are done, we are left with circumstances and memories. The circumstances are unarguable, so we know that somehow, certain things must have happened to account for the results of the past. But what really happened? There is always room for interpretation, and our memories are the way we choose to interpret the event.

The ninja were interested in results. They learned that part of generating results is taking the right perspective. How does one develop the right perspective? The ninja found that the way we tell the stories, the way we record our memories, determines our perspective. We vote for our perspective over time by the way we tell the story of our life.

If we always record our memories in mechanical and logical terms, then when we are faced with future difficulty, we will search for mechanical and logical solutions. If we tell our story as a sequence of struggles and failures, then we will expect and plan for a future sequence of struggles and failures. But what if the solution we needed was bigger and more elegant than we could understand? The secret power of the ninja lay in their ability to solve problems that were bigger than what logic could plan to overcome. They knew the secret of cultivating a mythic perspective.

It is in this way that the Kuji already exist inside of each person. Kuji manifests in our lives because we develop the capability to recognize the power, and then the capability to set things up to allow the power to surface. We don't make Strength happen. We let ourselves see Strength. Each story we hear helps us build an inner vision of what Strength looks like, so we can look for it in our own body, mind, and spirit.

Sometimes it helps to set aside the details and focus on the mythic story. A pure dream of Strength gives us the framework to see it peeking through the mask of everyday strife and to-do lists. Take in the stories as descriptions of how Strength might show up for you. Enjoy the dream, and then find Strength in your own life in Vajra time.

CHAPTER 10

Hanzo's Journey: Prologue

"Since the dawn of time, there have been men who chased legends, men who scoffed at legends, and men who became legends. The first are the true believers, who imagine themselves loyal by holding the faith, but who never become the object of their faith, always yearning for a time long past. The second are the intellectuals, the scholars, who imagine themselves the smartest, the holders of special knowledge, but who cannot put their knowledge to use, always yearning for a more perfect time to act. Lastly are the conquerors, the ones who strive boldly, who tackle the ambiguities of life and the terror of personal power. Their path is the least comfortable of all, painfully aware of lack, yet they become the very source of faith and knowledge."

Hanzo set down the scroll for a moment, and the last few words hung heavy in the air. "The source of faith and knowledge," he whispered again. "What is it?"

Beneath the kanji characters already read was a simple drawing of a mountain in the center of an island. The caption read "The Great Mt. Meru, center of the universe."

He had heard of the legend of Mt. Meru, the mountain that holds up the universe and the home of the gods. Many of the great heroes of the past were said to have visited Mt. Meru and received personal instruction in the kuji, the nine mystical powers of the ninja. He had often dreamed of learning such powers instead of merely memorizing sutra passages and quotations from past Masters. The stories never included an actual location for the mountain, however.

"You don't need to think about the scrolls. Just copy them," said the Temple Master from behind him.

Hanzo jumped and snatched up his brush. "Yes, sir. Sorry, sir." He quickly shuffled the Mt. Meru scroll behind some others.

The Master was not so easily fooled. "What is it that has you so excited, son?" He reached past Hanzo and pulled the exact scroll out from the center of the stack.

"It's the Mt. Meru scroll, sir," Hanzo said, looking down as the Master unfurled it.

"What about it?"

"Just… do you think it's an actual place?" Hanzo looked up carefully, suddenly aware that he had asked the master a direct question, and one that could be a challenge to authority. He awaited a blow.

The Master did not strike him. "Mt. Meru is real. The Founder retrieved the Teachings from the summit, battling numerous demons to do so. Everything we have is built on Mt. Meru, and that's why it is the center of the Universe."

Hanzo wanted to ask if he could visit Mt. Meru, see what the Founder saw, but it seemed blasphemous. He tried to blot the thought out quickly, before the Master could read him, but it was too late. Again he awaited the blow for incorrect thought.

The Master merely raised an eyebrow. "I can see that you will be useless to me until this is resolved. Go talk to the Archivist."

"Sir, I'm sorry, I will work hard…"

"GO!" he shouted, and Hanzo leapt to his feet and scurried out of the room.

He couldn't believe the Master didn't hit him. The fate awaiting him at the Archivist must be far worse, he reasoned. He wondered if he would be pilloried for his thoughts.

The Archivist sat in his small office at the end of the temple library, buried in scrolls recently returned from China or on loan from other temples around Japan. His job was to make sense of the overwhelming variety of teachings, categorizing them according to the intent of the Founder. Hanzo then copied the materials for the local library. They had spoken only rarely, when Hanzo needed help interpreting an obscure character or reading a damaged scroll. The Archivist was always difficult.

Hanzo bowed just outside the open door to the office and took up a waiting position within view. As usual, the Archivist completely ignored him for several minutes, giving Hanzo a welcome opportunity to count his breaths and try to figure out what he was going to say.

Finally, with an irritated grunt, the Archivist looked up from his work and glared at Hanzo. "What?"

"Sir, the Master told me I should speak with you," said Hanzo carefully.

The Archivist merely waved his hand impatiently at Hanzo, indicating he should get on with his purpose.

"And so, here I am. Sir, it's about the Mt. Meru scroll," Hanzo continued.

"What about it?"

"I asked the Master if Mt. Meru is real, and he said I should ask you." Hanzo carefully avoided mentioning the Master's expressed opinion.

"Real? Of course it isn't real. It's a metaphor. Do you know what a metaphor is, boy?"

"Yes, sir. It's a fiction told to make a point or express an idea. Not exactly a lie, so long as everyone knows it's fiction."

The Archivist looked surprised, but quickly masked it. "Yes, that's right. Which puts Mt. Meru right on the edge of being a lie, since a number of people are confused about it. There is no center of the universe as a physical place, because the universe goes on forever, and so it can't have a center."

"Yes, sir," said Hanzo, although he wasn't sure he agreed. "But the scroll is so specific about it. It shows Mt. Meru on that island, in the ocean. Why does it show it so specifically if it's only a metaphor? It looks like a real place."

"It's just art, Hanzo. Art and metaphor. The scroll also says that you should not chase after legends."

"And then it says you should go and become a legend!" he said impulsively, and then regretted it deeply as visions of punishment danced through his mind.

The Archivist drew back. "The Master was right. You have some ideas in your head that are immune to reason. We could beat you into silence, and perhaps we should, but it would accomplish nothing with regard to your insubordination. There is only one solution."

Hanzo cowered as the Archivist reached down behind his desk. He produced a bag that clinked on the desk with the distinct sound of gold coins. "Take these down to the wharfs," he said, "and ask every fisherman you can find for passage to Mt. Meru. If you can find even one who agrees, take him up on it. If you survive and return to us, we can get back to work."

Hanzo stared at the money bag like it was a snake. He had never held so much money. He realized that the Archivist was absolutely serious, and that he was expelled until he completed this task. Wordlessly, he scooped up the bag and left the office to gather his personal belongings.

It was worse than being pilloried.

CHAPTER 11

Hanzo's Journey: Strength

It was easy for Hanzo to carry everything he owned on his back. Although it was late in the afternoon when he was sent away, he left the temple right away, descending the mountain pathways as dusk fell and sleeping in a farmer's field near the base. The next morning he woke naturally with the sun, and for the first time in years, enjoyed freedom from his morning chores. He smiled as he stretched and then took himself through his daily prostrations, chants, and meditations.

By the time he set out again he had a spring in his step. This adventure, funded by the temple, might be a wonderful little journey. He reflected that perhaps this was actually his reward for his years of hard work.

Lunchtime arrived as he approached the fishing village, and he realized that he had no food. Luckily, the bag of gold was more than ample to cover the cost of a meal, so he treated himself to some very fresh fish and rice, packing additional rice in his traveling bundle for a meal later. It was mid-afternoon before he worked up the nerve to approach the tough looking fishermen at the wharfside.

Most of them were laughing as he approached, before he even opened his mouth. He was so obviously a temple assistant, no way to hide it, and they considered him soft and naïve in comparison to their sea-faring lives. When he asked about Mt. Meru, they merely chuckled or looked away, leaving him waiting without a reply.

By the tenth encounter, word of his mission had spread ahead of him. "No Mt. Meru here!" they guffawed as he approached. "We deal in fish and rice on the table, not ninja fairytales! Go home to your temple, boy, and tell the priests to pray for better harvests."

As evening approached, Hanzo decided that this trip was his punishment after all. The Master and the Archivist clearly knew what would result down here, and that he would be forced to return to them humbled, aware of his station and destiny in life. He briefly considered simply running away with the bag of gold, trying to start a life somewhere with it, but he hadn't the slightest idea how to do such a thing. He resigned himself to obediently completing the assigned exercise and returning at first light the next day.

It was a great relief when he was rejected at the last working wharf. He didn't mind the bits of food and crude jokes they threw at him. He knew he would never see these people again. He wandered down to a broken wharf, too rickety to be used for work now, and took advantage of his slight frame and excellent balance by walking along the single strong remaining beam out to the end. He sat down on the end, dangled his feet over the water, and took out the rice ball he had set aside earlier.

He took only a single bite, staring into the sunset, when a deep voice rumbled behind him. "What business do you have at Mt. Meru?"

He turned around on the narrow beam to encounter an absurdly large man standing behind him. How could such a person even be supported here, let alone sneak up so quietly? The man was at least a foot taller than the average worker here, with wild hair surrounding his head like a mane, horrible crooked teeth, and one eye missing under a mass of scar tissue. Still, despite his lack of grooming, he was strong and radiated health and power. "Uh, sir? Do you know the way to Mt. Meru?" Hanzo felt this must be some kind of trick.

"Of course I do, but Mt. Meru swallows fools. What makes you think you could survive such a place?" came the intimidating reply.

"Er… I don't know if I could, truth be told, but my Master told me to seek passage to Mt. Meru, and if anyone could provide it, I was to go immediately."

The strange man leaned down over Hanzo, sniffing the air like an animal. Hanzo could feel heat radiating from the man's body, as if a furnace were concealed inside his substantial torso. "Can you pay?" he rumbled.

"Yes, sir, I can pay." Hanzo produced the bag of gold, hoping the man would simply steal it and leave.

The man snatched the bag of gold, weighed it in his hands for a moment, and then nodded as he tucked it inside his vest. "Very well. Let us go." He turned and walked back down the beam toward shore with a grace that looked unnatural on such a mountainous body.

Alarm coursed through Hanzo. "Wait, what? Really?"

The man paused and shot him a glare. "Are you not obligated by your vows? Get up, or I'll tie you up and place you in the hold myself!"

Hanzo paled. Surely his life was coming to an end. He wondered what the man could want with him beyond just the money. It couldn't be good. His sense of terror collided with his sense of piety, and a kind of helplessness in the face of so much power. What could he do? He got up and followed the stranger.

The man walked back past the working wharfs of the men who had ridiculed Hanzo earlier. They seemed to know the giant, falling silent and averting their eyes as he passed. One of them made brief eye contact with Hanzo, shaking his head in pity.

They came at last to a barge moored at the other edge of the village. It was covered in smoldering garbage, and horrible smelling smoke wafted toward him. It didn't look like an ocean-going vessel in the slightest, but the stranger had rigged a sail to an awkward mast protruding from the center. The whole gave the impression of sailing a rotting island.

Hanzo was mortified, but felt as though it was not his decision to make. He followed the man obediently to the two-story cabin house, and the giant pushed away from the shore with a pole that was almost an entire log. Hanzo was afraid even to ask the man's name, afraid to know anything about him.

The sun set over the land behind them as they drifted out to sea. The ocean breezes helped dissipate the smell of rot and burning, and sitting on the floor of the cabin house, Hanzo finally overcame his shock enough to ask a question. "How long to Mt. Meru?"

"Go to sleep," the man replied. "I'll wake you when you arrive."

Suddenly all the fear drained out of Hanzo and he was overcome by a great fatigue. The day had been more than strange, and now his fate was in the hands of this powerful and eccentric one. There was nothing more to see until arrival.

Hanzo awoke with a gasp, unable to remember actually falling asleep. The giant was nowhere around, and he stepped out onto the deck to see that the barge was moored to a small pier at the base of a massive mountain-island jutting out of the ocean. A footpath from the pier ascended the island through low grasses, and there seemed to be no other course of action but to take it.

"This can't really be Mt. Meru," Hanzo said to himself as he stepped onto the pier. "Surely the man is a pirate or worse, playing a trick on me. I can't really be on the shores of the gods." He took one last look back at the barge. The garbage pile had burned down substantially, and sticking out of it were a number of strange objects. It took him a moment to realize that they were charred human limbs.

A strange numbness crept over him. He should have been horrified, but he felt like he had used up all the horror he could muster. He thought instead that he must be dead already, and these visions were mere illusions of the time between lives.

"I wonder when I died?" he said aloud. "I guess it doesn't matter. According to the Master, all of this is passing fantasy until I find my next life." He looked out at the calm ocean and felt the warm of the sun. It felt so real. He sighed. "I am nowhere near enlightenment. I may as well explore, while I wait."

He took the footpath. It was a winding and steep path, but somehow he didn't find himself getting tired. As he went higher up the mountain, the terrain changed gradually to forest, and then to exposed rock. He lost sight of the summit as he got closer, able only to see the next boulder that he would have to go around to proceed.

It was for this reason that the crystal temple appeared to him all at once. He rounded a boulder and found himself staring at an impossible fortress, seven stories tall and carved out of the purest quartz. The great columns supporting the massive roof soared upward, decorated on every surface with intricate abstract carvings. The gaping entrance was large enough for an army to ride into all at once.

If he didn't believe himself already dead and dreaming, he could never have moved from that spot. It was only the sense of nothing to lose that allowed him to move toward the entrance. The interior was even more fabulous. Curtains made of jewels decorated the walls, incense floated on the air, and heavenly music wafted in from unknown quarters. The main hall extended deeply into the mountain, and he walked down it so far that he expected it to get dark, but the walls themselves gave off a gentle glow.

At last he reached a massive stone staircase that led to a huge platform of solid jade. Atop the platform was a throne the size of a small building, a throne for a god. A sword the size of a horse sat next to the throne, with a massive thunderbolt-wand handle.

It suddenly struck him that dead or not, this was absolutely real. He was sitting in the home of one of the gods. The massive secret Sanskrit letter carved into the jade altar confirmed that he was in the abode of the great wrathful King of Light, Fudo Myo'o.

Hanzo began to quake with fear. It was all obvious in retrospect. The bargeman had been a manifestation of Fudo Myo'o, come to collect him from that wharf. He dropped into a full prostration on the ground and called out, "Great King of Light, all-powerful Fudo Myo'o, I do not know why you have brought me here. I lack even the power to endure your presence. Please, if I am not dead already, do not kill me. I will return to my temple and work hard for my Master."

The crystal floor rumbled beneath him, like the beginning of an earthquake. The music that had been so pleasant took on a more urgent tone, and then the conch-shell horns that call together military and prayer formations sounded all around him. The din was overwhelming, all consuming, and he glanced up to see the sword beginning to glow red.

"Great Noble One, I am not ready! I have more to do in this life! Give me another chance!" Hanzo called out in a panic. "Please, grant me your strength and return me to the world, so I can help both myself and others!"

The rumblings and horns only increased, and flames began to lick around the outside of the massive sword. Hanzo began to shake, and he pulled off his traveling pack and dug out the bit of rice he still had. Quickly shaping it into a ball, he placed it on the jade block, bowing his head. "Please, Great One, I give you all my food. I have already given you all my wealth. I give you all my spirit. Please assist me!"

The noise rose to a crescendo, and Hanzo felt certain that if Fudo Myo'o actually appeared, his heart would stop. He would simply expire on the spot from the stress. The sword burst into flames and a wave of heat passed over his body.

Suddenly he felt a surge of strength and jumped to his feet. "I won't die here! I won't!" he declared. He grabbed his pack, leaving the rice ball, and shouted one last exhortation to the power gathering around him. "Great One, I leave you my offering, and now I run!"

He sprinted down the hallway with a speed he had never known before. The jeweled walls of the crystal palace flew by on each side of him, and he burst into the sunlight outside. The whole mountain was rumbling, a volcano building to an eruption, and he dashed down the footpath to the barge. Leaping onto the barge, he stared at the log the giant had used to push off from the wharf in the fishing village. It was bigger than his whole body, surely impossible to lift, but as the mountain rumbled behind him, he found a new strength and wielded the log.

He pushed into the sand beneath the shallow water by the pier, and to his surprise, the heavy barge yielded. He drifted gradually away from the dock, poling with the log until he couldn't reach the bottom. The volcano built power and then erupted with a massive burst of lava, shooting burning rocks out of the top. As they crashed into the ocean all around him, they sizzled and hissed, creating a steamy fog that obscured sight in any direction.

Soon he could hardly tell that the barge was moving at all. All sights were surrounded by the fog, and all sound was consumed by the roaring fury of the volcano, now invisible behind its own veil of heat and water.

Hanzo sat down heavily on the deck, his senses and sensibilities overwhelmed. Again the great fatigue overtook him, and he slept.

Again he awoke suddenly in the cabin house of the barge. He sat up, rubbed his eyes, and stepped out onto the deck. The barge was right in the same place as when he first set foot on it, at the edge of town. The only clue to how much time had passed was that the garbage and human corpses that had been smoldering on the barge before were burned to ashes now. "How long would that take? And why is the boat intact if it burned so hotly?"

The first tendrils of dawn were just beginning to creep over the ocean horizon, and the only people about were the fishermen on the wharfs, preparing for the day. Hanzo couldn't help but wonder if the whole Mt. Meru experience were merely a dream. Maybe somehow he came down to this garbage barge, fell victim to the toxic fumes, and spent a few delirious days passed out in the cabin house until the cargo burnt itself out.

He checked his belongings. The gold and the rice ball were gone. His stomach growled in protest, and he realized it would be a long walk back with no breakfast. "I'd better get moving. At least I have an interesting story to share. Maybe the Master can help me understand what has happened."

He stepped onto land and walked toward the center of the village. The fishermen averted their eyes, as when he walked with the giant, so much so that he had to stop and look over his shoulder twice. No snarling giant was visible behind him, so he approached one of the men to investigate their strange reaction.

"Sir, if I may ask, how are you doing this morning?"

The fisherman looked up from his ropes. "I'm so sorry," he said. "Here, take this." He produced a rice ball from his pocket and offered it.

Hanzo's stomach compelled him to accept it. "Thank you, sir. I am hungry."

"Your Master was a good man. I hope you find your new home quickly," the man said, glancing at the horizon briefly before looking down at his ropes again.

Hanzo spun around in alarm and stared at his distant mountain home. With dawn gaining momentum, he could now make out the column of smoke from the temple area. Without another word to the fisherman, he took off in a panicked run.

His panic could only carry him a mile or so before exhaustion broke the spell. Well outside the village, he collapsed on the side of the road, tears filling his eyes and fear his heart. "What happened?" he yelled at the sky. "What is going on?" The sky cruelly refused to answer.

He shook and shivered, and then ate the rice ball to bring some stability to his body and mind. In doing so, he remembered his daily practice, and commenced it right where he had fallen. Each statement in the practice took on heavier meaning than ever before, as he reminded himself that life is suffering, caused by attachment, and that freedom from suffering means seeing things as they really are. He praised and invoked the various patron gods of his order, and his own Master and his extended lineage back to the Founder. Finally, he fortified himself with protection mantra, and dedicated his efforts to the good of all.

When he finally stood up he felt strong again, ready to face things. He still felt the bewilderment of a life turned upside down for reasons beyond his understanding, but he was ready to explore the circumstance and see what could be done. He set off for the temple at a quick but deliberate pace.

Whenever his mind offered up nightmarish visions based on fear, he invoked Fudo Myo'o to chase those visions away and fortify him with supernatural strength. When at last he reached the temple site late in the afternoon, and witnessed firsthand the collapsed buildings and smoldering wreckage, his heart was set in a grim clarity. This was no accident. Someone of great power had come and destroyed the temple.

He wanted to search for survivors, but he knew there would be none. Instead he looked for the traditional declaration scroll, probably pinned to a tree nearby, explaining the reasons for the attack. He found it and read it aloud. "For the crimes of harboring ninja and supporting rebellion, this temple's license is officially declared invalid." It was signed by the local warlord Seiji.

Rage filled Hanzo. Seiji had no right to destroy the temple and the sacred work of generations. The scrolls he had spent his life copying were now ash, and his mentors were dead. The bright wisdom of this temple was snuffed out. "There are no ninja here!" he yelled at the scroll proclaiming the temple's sentence. "I wish there had been! Maybe then they could have prevented your monstrous act! You're looking for a rebellion? I've got one for you right here!"

He spun around in a circle, frustrated, trying to vent the energy but having no way to do so. Finally he decided to put the energy to good use, digging through the ruins to see what could be salvaged. He oriented himself and went to his own quarters, but they had burned hotly and were simply piles of charcoal. The library was similarly gone, which was unsurprising given all the scrolls there. He hoped that the warlord had at least stolen the scrolls so they wouldn't be lost forever.

The Archivist's office was charred but still somewhat structurally intact. It looked rickety, but it still held the shape of a building. He stepped carefully inside and found the Archivist's burned body face down behind his desk, back full of arrows. He felt compassion for the man for the first time, realizing that a greater enemy makes lesser tormentors into friends.

He rolled the Archivist over to look at his face, and found it remarkably composed. Perhaps the old man had taken in some spiritual lessons over the years. His hands were clasping his kimono tightly closed, however, and not formed in the traditional mudra shape preparing for death. It seemed out of place, all other things considered, and while Hanzo did not want to disturb the dead unduly, he gently moved the man's hands into the correct shape. The kimono fell open as he did so, revealing a scroll.

"Of all these ancient writings, what was so important to save, old friend?" he said, taking the scroll and unfurling it. He was chilled to see that the first characters were his name.

"Hanzo, the warlord Seiji has come to destroy us. He is taking the Master to his compound for interrogation, believing him to be a ninja. Consider that much of what you hear, and even some of what you see, is untrue, but consider also that rumors arise for reasons. Seek truth always."

Hanzo fell away from the body, processing the news. Of all the incredibly important works in the library and the Archivist's office, he chose only to preserve this letter. Somehow he knew that Hanzo would find it, and it seemed the hopes of the Master were pinned on Hanzo now. Did they send him away, knowing of the coming attack? Did they know what he saw in his vision of Mt. Meru?

His reverie was interrupted by the sound of creaking and then splintering wood. In a single moment, the whole office lost structural stability around him and came crashing down. A heavy wood beam pinned Hanzo to the floor as debris rained down and buried him.

The movement stopped, and he found himself uninjured, but unable to move, sealed in a dark tomb beside the body of the Archivist. He struggled once and then again against the weight, but it was far beyond him.

All of the heroic hope of the previous moment seemed suppressed by the massive weight. This place of death had pulled him into its trap, and now he was caught like a rabbit in a snare. What of the hopes of the Master? What of the faith that they had put in him? Now he had failed before even beginning.

Deep in the earth he heard and then felt a rumbling. The horses of a hunting party? Distantly a battlefield horn sounded. His hopes rose that someone was coming to save him, but the rumbling subsided and the horn didn't sound again. Despair overtook him for a moment, and then turned to anger.

"Why?" he shouted from under the rubble. "Why should I have all these experiences, and be led here, only to die?"

The earth rumbled in reply.

"What is that supposed to mean?" he yelled again. He shoved on the beam, but it wouldn't budge. "Damn it!"

The rumbling increased. His mind touched the same rumbling in the memory of Mt. Meru.

"If no man will save me, I will do it myself. Fudo Myo'o, I need your power now. Help me lift the beam."

The rumbling increased again. He felt it in his tissues and bones, vibrating strength into him. He adjusted his position slightly under the beam for leverage. "Fudo Myo'o, hear me and help! Come on!"

Another horn sounded in the distance, and the rumbling built intensely. Hanzo felt a surge of power move through his body, as when he ran from Mt. Meru's eruption, and the beam yielded slightly. He hesitated not a moment, adjusting his body as it yielded and shoving harder, keeping the momentum going. The mass shifted off to the side, and the small debris with it, until suddenly he was free. He burst out of the ashes with a triumphant shout. "Come on!"

He looked around for the horses, but the forest was silent. No horns sounded, no shouts were audible. He picked himself out of the ruins and brushed off the ashes. "I have survived all this for a reason," he said to the forest. "I will rescue the Master. Maybe there is a ninja in this temple after all."

Hanzo picked through the ruins for any salvageable supplies, but came away with just a handful of coins and a heavy coat. The Archivist's body was thoroughly buried under the remains of his office, so rather than dig him out and re-bury him, he carried rocks to the site and created a grave out of the office. It seemed appropriate for the Archivist to go into the afterlife with his office.

He found other bodies too, and said a prayer over each, but in the interest of the Master, he decided not to linger for days burying the dead and erecting proper memorials. That would have to wait. As the dark of the night thoroughly overtook the site, and he could search no longer, he curled up in the heavy coat in the nearby forest and fell into a dreamless sleep.

The next morning he awoke naturally, for the first time since the sunny field at the beginning of this journey. He moved through his daily practice quickly, the old familiar rituals warming up his brain and body. He said a last prayer over the entire temple site before setting out for the fishing village again to see what help he could gather.

He arrived at the village that afternoon to find a farmer's market in progress. Along with the usual vendors and performers, there was a carnival booth that attracted his attention with a sign that read "The Sword of Fudo Myo'o." The man running the booth had a giant sword, taller than the average man, of the same style he had seen on Mt. Meru. He had a length of rope several feet long and as thick as a horse, some kind of specialty rope used to moor battleships. The challenge was to cut the rope with the sword in a single sweep.

The rope was covered with little dents and slices all over the length, but no one had come even close to cutting through it with the giant sword. It cost two coins to try, but success meant one hundred coins.

Hanzo stepped up the booth and put down his two coins. "I'd like to try, sir."

The con man was happy to oblige, but nearby voices snickered. The sword probably weighed more than Hanzo. One of the voices cat-called, "Forget it, boy! Just give me your two coins and you'll at least avoid pulling your back out."

Hanzo turned around to see the speaker and discovered a samurai lounging with two friends on hay bales. Obviously drunk, the man also wore the insignia of the warlord Seiji. Hanzo's eyes flashed, but he knew he had to control himself. These men had the power to kill him here in the market and walk away freely.

"A side bet, then!" he called back. "Your horse if I can do it."

People nearby were already tuning in to the showdown, and several of them gasped at the audacity of Hanzo's challenge. The samurai however laughed and raised his mug at Hanzo.

"Nice try, boy. What could you possibly offer for your side of that bet?"

Hanzo bowed instinctively while his mind raced for an answer. He had been a servant his whole life. "My servitude," he replied. It was the only bargaining chip he had.

The other samurai laughed now and poked their friend, making lewd comments. Temple boys had a certain reputation, and though he would die before he would submit to these killers, he didn't correct their assumptions. The man took a gulp of his drink and shouted back. "You've got it, boy. Grasp my sword and show us your talent!" The crowd roared at the innuendo.

He turned his back on them and stepped up to the challenge. The sword was indeed incredibly heavy and he could barely lift the handle off the ground. He dragged it into position, the blade dragging in the dirt behind him. The crowd gathered around shouted both encouragement and derision. "Show us what you're made of!" came one voice. "You'll never manage!" called another.

He closed his eyes and directed his attention inward, whispering his prayer. "Great and Noble Fudo Myo'o, I need to win this challenge, not only for my life, but for the life of my Master and the prosperity of all those who rely on the wisdom of the Teachers. Please assist me."

He heard the rumbling in the ground again, and this time he knew what it was. He knew the crowd couldn't hear it, wouldn't recognize it, but he tuned in the rumbling sound and feeling and let it build up inside. He flexed his knees deeply and placed the dull iron of the blade on his hip. When the power surged up through him from the ground he launched upward with his legs. The sword surged high, higher even than he expected, and then fell down like an executioner's axe. He waited just a moment as it gathered momentum toward the rope, and then flexed his knees again, dropping his weight into the sword just as its natural weight dropped onto the target.

The rope parted with the loud snap from the tension holding it out, and the blade thudded into the ground. For a moment, the only sound was Hanzo's breath, heaving from exertion, and then the crowd erupted in cheers. He turned around to find the samurai on his feet, his face turning red with rage.

Hanzo had won the bet, but he knew that the man was close to killing him. He became extraordinarily polite. "Great warrior," he said, addressing the samurai, "my victory was beginner's luck only. I'm sure you could do the same ten times over. Please excuse me. I must go to buy medicine for my ailing Master with the gold. Please leave the horse for me at the inn, that I may deliver the medicine when I am back." The statement was true, in a way, and he hoped that it sounded honorable enough that the samurai would feel social pressure not to murder him on the spot.

The man blinked twice, then sat back down heavily and waved his drink at him in a vague gesture of acknowledgment. Hanzo bowed to him, took the bag of gold coins from the vendor, and departed immediately.

Fudo Myo'o had saved him twice now, and he knew what he had to do. He returned to the wharf where he left the barge, hoping to take it back to Mt. Meru and seek the advice of the deity. To his surprise, the barge was not there, but the giant was, sitting on the end of the wharf fishing. He looked up at Hanzo's approach.

"Hanzo!" he called. "How did you like your trip to Mt. Meru?"

It was such an outrageous thing to shout that Hanzo looked around wildly, to see what others might think. No one was particularly close, nor paying any special attention, but Hanzo hurried down to the end of the wharf in hopes of continuing the conversation more quietly.

"Sir! I need to return. I desperately need the power of the Great King."

"Sure, sure you do," said the giant, nodding, "but you don't need to go back to Mt. Meru to get it. Now that you've visited his temple, you can call on him anytime you need."

Hanzo's eyes widened. Had the man somehow witnessed the marketplace scene, or his moment of strength at the temple? "Sir? My Master is in great danger. I need to know how to save him."

"Nonsense!" the giant rumbled. "You already know what to do. You simply need to believe you can do it." Hanzo sat in silence, not daring to disagree, and the imposing man continued. "You have your gold for supplies, and soon you'll have your horse. What you need is a practice, a way to call up the power of Fudo Myo'o at will, without pushing yourself into reckless crisis to reach it." He turned and poked Hanzo with one meaty finger. "Fudo Myo'o respects bravery, but no one can save a fool."

The man turned and looked out at the horizon of the ocean. Hanzo did the same, and a moment of silence passed where he couldn't think of a single thing to say.

"If you want to learn, meet me here at sundown tonight. I will teach you what you need to know now. The rest you will discover for yourself."

"What will I owe you for this training?" asked Hanzo.

"Oh, you'll earn the teachings," the man said cryptically, "but gold is not the currency. Keep your gold for provisions, do your shopping, and return if you really want to save your Master. Otherwise, take the gold and the horse, flee south, and make a new life, forgetting all the strange and difficult times. It's your choice to make."

"But how can I know what to do? How is it even possible for a scribe such as myself to…" Hanzo turned back toward the man as he spoke, and realized he was gone. He hung in the silence, looked around in all directions, and accepted the seemingly impossible truth that the man could vanish so swiftly. He let out his breath in a sigh and stared at the horizon again. How indeed could any of this be true?

As surreal as the situation was, the idea of running from it seemed even less plausible. Returning to town, he found a horse waiting for him at the inn. He was not surprised that it was not the samurai's warhorse but a simple farming horse, purchased, or maybe commandeered, from a local. The horse was healthy enough to serve his needs. He took it to the market and began loading it up with supplies.

After stocking up for the several day's ride to Seiji's fortress, Hanzo left his horse at the inn with his supplies and returned to the dock area at sundown as instructed. The giant was waiting.

"I see your choice. Very well. Training begins immediately. The power of Fudo Myo'o is called *Rin*, the power of strength." The man twisted his enormous fingers together into a special hand shape. "This mudra channels the power of *Rin*, at the level of the body."

Hanzo attempted the mudra hand posture, taking a couple of attempts to get it right. The man waited for him to get it, and then showed him how to synchronize his breathing with it, pushing the mudra up overhead, pulling it back to center, and then pushing it out in front of the chest. "Imagine the power of Fudo Myo'o surging through you as you breathe," he said, and they practiced together for a few minutes.

Hanzo found it easy enough, easier than the austere meditation training he had received at the temple. He followed along and hoped the deity was looking kindly on his practice.

"Now," the man shouted, "we add the mantra! *Namaku samanda bazaradan senda maka roshina sowataya un tarata kan man*!"

Hanzo jumped when the ancient words were shouted. They were utterly foreign, not Japanese words, but the giant kept shouting them with each breath. After a few times, he recognized the rhythms of the ancient language from India, in which the oldest scrolls were written. He didn't know what the words meant, but he could make the sounds. After several attempts, he could follow along, shouting the words along with the giant.

As they shouted, the pace and intensity of their shouts increased, gradually building into a frenzy. Hanzo could feel himself getting more excited, more agitated, as the energy built. Just when he thought he couldn't take it anymore, the giant changed his inflection on the next shout. The mantra ended with a definitive finality, and Hanzo fell silent along with the man.

The silence that followed was deafening. He felt like the dock was drifting out into the sea, or he was drifting out of his own body. He wondered briefly if the whole town had heard them, but no one was running to investigate. He could feel the power in his body, especially in his hands, as he released the mudra hand posture and relaxed into a meditative rest position.

After the silence soaked in and the sound of the water lapping against the dock came back into the foreground, the man turned to Hanzo. "That is the practice. Remember it well and follow me." He stood up and strode down the dock.

Hanzo followed wordlessly as they ascended a trail up the cliff bordering the ocean. It wasn't long before they were looking down nearly 100 feet into the waves crashing into the rocks. The giant produced a rope and tied it around Hanzo's chest, the rope trailing from behind.

"You're going to lower me down the cliff?" asked Hanzo.

"No. I'm just going to help you to get a better view," chuckled the man. He put a hand on Hanzo's back and guided him to the edge of the cliff. "I have the rope. Lean out over the edge."

Hanzo looked at him in surprise. "Really?"

"You think I'll drop you?"

"No!" Hanzo said. "It's just…" He trailed off. There was little point in arguing. It just came down to whether he would follow this teacher or not. He took a deep breath and leaned out slightly.

"More!" came the shout from behind him, and he leaned forward further. "Keep going!" said the man.

Soon he was leaning way out over the cliff, staring at the water, the rocks, and the sky. His heart pounded in his chest. The man could have killed Hanzo any time he wanted before now, and he was more than strong enough to hold him, but despite that, the visual of the drop was so intense that his body responded to the fear. He felt his gut tighten and his breath catch.

"Now what?" he forced out.

"Now you practice! Mudra and mantra!" shouted the man. "*Namaku samanda bazaradan senda maka roshina sowataya un tarata kan man!*"

Hanzo forced a breath into his body, his chest straining against the rope. He tried to shout the manta, but on the first breath it came out squeaky and weak. He felt foolish for a moment, and then the embarrassment turned to anger. The second mantra came out in a normal voice, and the third one came out in a roar.

The giant shouted the mantra out behind him, and as Hanzo yelled into the wind, his hands came together in the mudra. He felt a ball of energy building up in his chest, and suddenly he realized he wasn't afraid anymore. He felt free and powerful, despite the visual threat, and the fear in his gut converted into a sense of confidence.

Hanzo lost track of time, but he knew it was over when the giant reeled him in. He let the mantra dissipate, relaxed his hands out of the mudra, and stared out at the ocean. He felt like a capable adult for the first time, ready to begin his adventure. He turned around to face the giant, half expecting him to be somehow vanished.

Instead he was standing right behind him. "Very good. That's the feeling. Now the test. You'll spend the night in the cave."

"What cave?" asked Hanzo.

The giant merely shoved him forward, and Hanzo's arms windmilled as he went over the edge of the cliff, despite the confidence he had felt moments before. He caught on the rope immediately, hanging in space just over the edge. "The cave is below. I'll lower you to it and return in the morning. Practice well, and you will survive." He lowered Hanzo down to a platform halfway to the sea, slick with spray and exposed to the wind.

Hanzo crouched on the platform, and then scrambled into the cave, seeking some kind of wind protection. The cave was not very deep, but he was able to find a corner in the side that allowed a small measure of protection.

Within minutes he was freezing cold. He pulled himself into a ball and began the practice before he lost confidence and the control of his thoughts. Shouting against the cold, time blurred. The cold seeped into his bones, until he could feel the sea-spray laden wind as if it were actual ice water pouring over his body. He fought against it, rocking involuntarily as he focused on the mantra, focused on visualizing the strength of Fudo Myo'o.

Water entered his nose, jolting him out of the practice. His eyes shot open and filled with icy water. He sputtered and gasped at the sudden immersion and staggered to his feet. Stumbling forward in the cave to get out of the pouring waterfall, he emerged in a crystal clear pool on the sunny slopes of Mt. Meru.

Hanzo forced himself across the pool to the sandy shore, soaking up the sunlight and convulsing in recovery. Mt. Meru towered above, the slopes that were once forest-covered scorched and ashen. The crystal palace was visible near the summit, but between Hanzo and there lay fields of hot coals, still burning from the eruption he witnessed on his last visit.

Hanzo looked down at his barefoot feet and back at the hot coals. He took a deep breath, stated the mantra boldly, and stepped from the shores of the icy pool to the burning path. "Keep moving!" he said to himself, and then launched into repetitions of the mantra. "*Namaku samanda bazaradan senda maka roshina sowataya un tarata kan man!*"

He moved swiftly over the coals, and though he could feel the heat, his feet did not burn. For a moment he thought perhaps the coals were merely an illusion, and he halted. In less than a second the heat built to intolerable levels, and he leapt back into action, chanting and walking.

He breathed a sigh of relief when he finally stepped onto the cool marble flooring of the impossible crystal palace. The angelic music, the beautiful architecture, and the sweet incense clouds billowing out of the halls soothed his mind and body. Still, he felt fear as he approached the jade altar and the massive thunderbolt sword.

"Fudo Myo'o, hear my request. I come for strength and training."

The building rumbled in reply. Hanzo felt his belly tighten and his breathing shorten. He consciously drew deeper breaths to stabilize his body and mind.

The rumbling grew louder, the floor moving beneath him, and he knew the deity was approaching. As before, the horns began to sound and the thunderbolt sword glowed until flames licked around the edges. This was where he lost his nerve before, but Hanzo was determined to stick it out this time. So much had happened since the last time he was here—he had lost his home temple, his Master, and most of his possessions. His old life was gone, and now it was time to find a new one, either metaphorically in this body or literally if he should die.

The crescendo of the horns was accompanied by the crashing of gongs, and the flames on the sword spread to the throne itself. Heat washed over him, but he held his ground, chanting the mantra and invoking the inner feeling of Fudo's strength that he had found in the temple ruins, the marketplace challenge, and the cliff edge by the sea.

The flames grew so intense and so bright that he was forced to look away for a moment, and that was the very second when he felt a vast presence enter the room. The music stopped, and the light ebbed slightly. He looked back at the throne to see the massive blue-skinned muscle-bound form of Fudo Myo'o. The deity gripped the thunderbolt sword and scowled at him with just one eye, the other closed in a squint. He looked fierce, even angry, but he did not attack. He rose from his throne and towered over Hanzo.

Hanzo continued to chant the mantra as he prostrated himself. After a prolonged bow where the deity did not strike him, he rose carefully and found the deity also rising from a deep bow. Both beings stood and stared, contemplating the meaning of the other.

The mantra died from Hanzo's lips now. He could feel the force of Fudo even without words, could see his strength even without action. He shifted his weight to the left, unconsciously, and the deity matched his movement. The deity flexed his sword arm, and Hanzo echoed the movement back. Slowly, like a dance, they began to move together in a slow and powerful choreography. Hanzo would offer a movement, and the deity would match it. Then Fudo would reply with a movement, and Hanzo would match it. He observed as carefully as he could, matching the details of footwork, hip alignment, the tempo of movement, and the bearing brought to it.

The conversation of movement gradually transmitted a sensation to Hanzo, a feeling of what it would be like to move like Fudo Myo'o, what it would be like to feel that way. From his side, Hanzo gradually proposed all of his awkward or nervous affectations, and one by one, the deity echoed them back with strength, power, and grace.

Not a word was said, but the teaching was clear. Hanzo had a momentary thrill, a reflection of his success at reaching the deity, and just at that moment, the being began to fade. Hanzo quickly pushed the thought out of his mind and returned to the dance. He admonished himself to be Fudo Myo'o, to be fully present with the Great King.

He sank into a kind of trance in the process. He lost track of who was leading each movement, until there seemed to be just a single mind guiding the process, with no particular leader or follower. He sank into the mind of Fudo Myo'o, and equally so, the deity sank into his mind.

At some point, he looked down at his hands and saw blue. He flexed his powerful muscles, wielded the flaming thunderbolt sword, and felt the rope lariat in his other hand. There was no difference anymore between Hanzo and Fudo Myo'o.

The dance came to a halt, and the one merged being stood still, contemplating itself in a giant round mirror across the throne room. He nodded to himself in approval and awareness. With nothing left to do, he folded his immortal power into meditation posture and closed his eyes.

"Is this real?" he thought to himself first. Then came, "What could that even mean? What could be more real?" He directed his mind into wordless and silent contemplation.

After a time, light shone through his eyelids and a warm sensation spread over his body. His mind was brought back to the feeling, and curiosity formed. He cracked his eyes open to see a fabulous blazing dawn over the ocean, and the first rays of the sun fell on him with surprising intensity for the early hour. He became aware of his body, and found it to be a human body, atop a cliff facing the sea.

Gradually his ordinary memories seeped back in. The giant and his rope were nowhere to be found. Hanzo stretched his cold body, and it ached in protest, but it seemed a distant and minor complaint. He wondered if the giant had been a hallucination, a manifestation of the deity, or simply a clever teacher-practitioner of Fudo Myo'o. Right away he knew it didn't matter. Fudo Myo'o lived inside him now. He had access to the strength of the Great King. He could feel it deep inside, ready anytime he needed it.

"What could be more real than this?" he said to himself.

Credits, Acknowledgments, and Contact

Living the Kuji experience is a grand adventure, and it is impossible without an entire community to provide context, support, and challenge. All the friends, training partners, and teachers who have helped me over the years have my gratitude, along with the event organizers who created venues to access these teachings. Special thanks also extend to those who created material used in the book: Kim Speek for instructional photographs, Keegan Shorrock for hand-modeling the mudra and creating the seed-syllable image used in chapter headings throughout, and SKH Inc. for the use of The Code of Mindful Action.

Appreciation and acknowledgement goes to Mary A. Stevens II, my partner and co-creator of the Boulder Quest Center dojo and community. Our adventures and efforts built the ultimate laboratory and playground for us to deepen our paths and discover our truths. We go forth stronger for having met.

Deepest appreciation for support of this book goes to my primary teacher, An-Shu Stephen K. Hayes, for countless conversations and teachings, far beyond what could be included in this book. He teaches tirelessly, endures my misconceptions at all stages of the path, and constantly challenges me to do much better than good enough. He is also a sincere and profound friend.

My own students must be acknowledged too, for it is in attempting to express what I think I know that I achieve the deepest relationship with my own understanding. I so appreciate the chance to teach.

Lastly, let us never forget what insights we gain via the long invisible lineage of departed teachers, the magic of passing strangers we may never know, and whatever transpersonal forces guide the emergence of this knowledge in our modern era. Wisdom comes from so many directions. In fact, even enemies and obstacle-makers along the way are to be thanked, for they make the heroic journey possible. Without someone to play the role of enemy, there is no battle, no victory, and no hero. To learn more about Kuji One or to arrange an in-person experience of the methods, please visit my teacher's website at: **www.StephenKHayes.com**